LEADING WOMEN

Elizabeth Warren

Democratic
Senator from
Massachusetts

JERI FREEDMAN

Cavendish
Square

New York

Published in 2018 by Cavendish Square Publishing, LLC
243 5th Avenue, Suite 136, New York, NY 10016

Copyright © 2018 by Cavendish Square Publishing, LLC

First Edition

Library of Congress Cataloging-in-Publication Data
Names: Freedman, Jeri, author.
Title: Elizabeth Warren : Democratic Senator from
Massachusetts / Jeri Freedman.
Description: New York : Cavendish Square Publishing, [2018] |
Series: Leading women | Includes bibliographical references and index.
Identifiers: LCCN 2016059794 (print) | LCCN 2017000069 (ebook) |
ISBN 9781502626998 (library bound) | ISBN 9781502627001 (E-book)
Subjects: LCSH: Warren, Elizabeth. |
Women legislators--United States--Biography--Juvenile literature. |
Legislators--United States--Biography--Juvenile literature. |
United States. Congress. Senate--Biography--Juvenile literature. |
United States--Politics and government--21st century--Juvenile literature.
Classification: LCC E901.1.W37 F75 2017 (print) | LCC E901.1.W37 (ebook) |
DDC 328.73092 [B] --dc23
LC record available at https://lccn.loc.gov/2016059794

Editorial Director: David McNamara
Editor: Tracey Maciejewski
Copy Editor: Nathan Heidelberger
Associate Art Director: Amy Greenan
Designer: Lindsey Auten
Production Coordinator: Karol Szymczuk
Photo Research: J8 Media

The photographs in this book are used by permission and through the courtesy of: Cover United States
Senate/Wikimedia Commons/File:Elizabeth Warren--Official 113th Congressional Portrait--.jpg/
CCO; pp. 4, 25, 60, 64 Boston Globe/Getty Images; p. 13 Brian Reading/Wikimedia Commons/
File:Ezekiel W. Cullen building 3.jpg/CC BY-SA 4.0; p. 16 Leif Skoogfors/Corbis Historical/Getty
Images; p. 30 Terry Ashe/The LIFE Images Collection/Getty Images; p. 36 Spencer Platt/Getty
Images; pp. 39, 56, 78 Bloomberg/Getty Images; p. 41 Charles Eshelman/WireImage/Getty Images;
p. 46 Brooks Kraft/Corbis Historical/Getty Images; p. 50 Chris Maddaloni/CQ-Roll Call Group/
Getty Images; p. 67 Brooks Kraft/Corbis News/Getty Images; p. 71 Saul Loeb/AFP/Getty Images;
p. 74 The Washington Post/Getty Images; p. 83 US Senate/Alamy Stock Photo.

Printed in the United States of America

CONTENTS

5   ONE: *On the Ragged Edge*

17 TWO: *Getting Started*

31 THREE: *Taking on the Banks*

47 FOUR: *Protecting the People*

61 FIVE: *The National Stage*

79 SIX: *What the Future Holds*

94 Timeline

96 Source Notes

101 Glossary

102 Further Information

104 Bibliography

110 Index

112 About the Author

CHAPTER ONE

On the Ragged Edge

Unlike many senators, Elizabeth Warren doesn't come from a wealthy or powerful family. According to Warren, "I grew up in a family on the ragged edge of the middle class."[1] She was born Elizabeth Herring in Oklahoma City, Oklahoma, on June 22, 1949, the youngest of Donald and Pauline Herring's four children. Her three brothers were much older than she, and all three served in the military. One brother made a permanent career in the military, another became a construction worker, and the third started a small business.

Elizabeth Warren's childhood home. Unlike many senators, she came from a modest background.

The Dust Bowl and the Great Depression

Elizabeth Warren's parents had lived through the Great Depression and the hard times of the Dust Bowl in Oklahoma. The Great Depression (1929–1939) was the worst and longest economic downturn in US history. It began with the stock market crash of October 1929, which led to the failure of a large number of banks and businesses. Unemployment rose as many companies failed and others cut back on workers. At its peak in 1933, thirteen to fifteen million Americans were unemployed and living on charity. The economy did not completely recover until World War II created a need for vast amounts of industrial production.

The Dust Bowl was the Great Plains region, a 150,000-square-mile (388,500-square-kilometer) area covering the Oklahoma and Texas panhandles and adjacent areas of Kansas, Colorado, and New Mexico. Devastated by drought during the Great Depression, ranches and farms failed, and the dry soil was swirled around by winds, creating dust storms. Nearly 60 percent of the population of the area left during this time.

Warren's parents often talked about their experiences in the Great Depression. According to Warren, "They talked about it, those were the stories that permeated my childhood, what it was like to have seven years of drought, what it was like when nobody had any money, what it was like when all your neighbors left to go to California or someplace where they thought there might be jobs."[2] Unlike some of their neighbors, Warren's parents stayed in Oklahoma.

Growing Up "Middle Class"

At the time Warren was born, her parents were struggling financially and often had a hard time making ends meet, but they considered themselves middle class, nonetheless. They firmly believed in education and insisted on using proper English, which they felt distinguished middle-class from lower-class people. Elizabeth took her first job when she was nine, babysitting for a family who lived across the street. At thirteen, she started working as a waitress in her aunt Bee's restaurant. She grew up feeling that, although no one in the family had much of anything, they all tried to look out for each other. Reflecting on her childhood in an interview with Harry Kreisler of the Institute of International Studies at the University of California, Berkeley, Warren said:

> *People who didn't have family or people who broke from their family, they were the true poor, they were the ones with nothing. As long as you had family, you had people who would make sure that you got fed one way or another. Family was about canning peaches, and canning peaches was about making sure that there'd at least be something come next November, when it was cold outside and there were no more crops coming in. Family is the heart of what it's about.*[3]

When Warren was twelve, her father suffered a heart attack while working on the family car. Medical treatment resulted in huge medical bills, and her father was unable to work for some time. When he was ready to return to work, his job selling carpet at Montgomery Ward was gone. Instead, the company offered him a position selling outdoor products such as lawn mowers and fences. He was only paid a commission when he sold an item, so he no longer brought in a regular salary. The family's car was repossessed. Warren's mother, who was fifty years old, went to work answering phones for Sears, at minimum wage, to bring in money to pay the mortgage on their house. Eventually, her father left his job at Montgomery Ward and became a maintenance man at an apartment building.

Growing up in this hardworking lower-middle-class family instilled in Warren the importance of hard work and taught her how easily a middle-class family's finances could be destroyed by a single catastrophic problem. She felt she lacked the intangible things that having enough money gave her classmates: confidence, a feeling of security, and family stability. When she was campaigning for the Senate, she described her family as "kind of hanging on at the edges by our fingernails."[4]

Warren credits the conditions in which she grew up with shaping her worldview. The stories she heard from her parents and the hardships her own family went through gave her **empathy** for the plight of other hardworking families who found themselves in financial trouble because of a sudden unforeseen crisis. She developed a lifelong commitment to helping middle- and working-class families struggling to get by like hers.

Warren was influenced by her teachers as well as her parents. She says:

I had wonderful teachers. I'm of that generation where there were only two things that a woman could do, if she wanted to do something other than stay home, and that was, she could become a nurse or she could become a teacher. And so, there were some awfully able women who taught me from grade school on, and what they opened me up to was the possibility that I, too, could be a teacher. And frankly, when I went off to college, the whole idea [was] that I could be a teacher. That's what I wanted to do. I just didn't quite know what kind of teacher I would end up becoming.[5]

Warren felt awkward in high school. She liked the academic side, but failed to fit in socially, despite joining groups like the school pep club (a group that does chants and cheers during school games, much like a cheerleading squad but without performing on the field). Warren says, "I wasn't any good at *high school*—parties, friends, football games."[6] Part of the problem was that, with a teenager's lack of perspective, she was certain that her family was the only one that struggled with their finances, and this made her feel self-conscious. She rarely made friends because she didn't want to have to invite them over and have them see her house.

Elizabeth started dating her first boyfriend, Jim Warren, when she was a thirteen-year-old high-school freshman and he was a seventeen-year-old junior. Both were on the debate team. However, the romance didn't last, and Jim Warren became Elizabeth's first breakup.

Achieving College

Elizabeth had skipped sixth grade, so when she was sixteen she was a senior in high school. Like many seniors, she started thinking about going to college. When her mother first realized this, she discouraged the idea, pointing out that they couldn't afford it, and that college-educated girls had a harder time finding a husband—still the major goal for young women at that time and place. Later, however, her mother relented, suggesting that if Warren wanted to go to college, she could attend one nearby while living at home and working part time. Warren has said that she suspects her mother expected her to go to college until she found a husband, and then quit. That wasn't what Warren had in mind, however.

Warren's plans for college were more ambitious, but going to college away from home required money. One solution would be to get a scholarship, but although she was a good student, she didn't have the top grades in her school, nor was she a talented athlete. What she did excel at was debating. She educated herself about topics she knew nothing about and could argue about them convincingly. Debating instilled a sense of self-discipline in her, teaching her to keep fighting rather than give up. More important, it gave her a shot at a college scholarship. From the guidance counselor's office at her school, she borrowed a book that described various colleges and found that Northwestern University in Chicago had a debate team and offered a scholarship in this area. A boy on the debate team at her high school told her that George Washington University in Washington, DC, also had a debate team and gave scholarships. Warren sent for applications from both universities.

Without letting her parents know her plan, she filled out the forms and returned them, only to find out that to qualify for a scholarship, she had to submit information on her parents' earnings. When she broached the subject to her parents, her mother continued to object, but her father insisted she be allowed to try. When she saw her parents' tax returns, she realized for the first time that—despite her mother's long-held position that they were middle class—the family was quite poor. Both schools accepted her. George Washington offered her a combination scholarship and student loan that provided room, board, and a bit of spending money, but the offer didn't quite cover all her needs. However, by working part time while going to school and full time over the summer, Warren was able to accrue enough money for the rest of her expenses. She majored in **speech pathology** and **audiology** (speech and hearing disorders) because she was interested in working with children who had brain injuries. According to Warren, "My mother responded to my news with equal parts pride and worry. She would say to friends: 'Well, she figured out how to go to college for free, so what could I say? But I don't know if she'll ever get married.'"[7]

Married Life

Her mother need not have worried, although marriage would turn out to be a mixed blessing for Elizabeth. In 1968, when she was nineteen, in her second year of college, Jim Warren again entered Elizabeth's life. With a good job at IBM and exuding confidence, he asked her to marry him, and Elizabeth agreed, dropping out of college to become his wife. The couple moved to Houston. Elizabeth took a temporary job, but she still wanted to become a teacher. Moreover, she had student loans that she needed to pay. If she became a teacher, the government would forgive some of those loans. So, she convinced her new husband that she should go back to school at the University of Houston.

In 1970, Elizabeth graduated from college. Shortly after, her husband was transferred by his company to a new job in New Jersey. There, at twenty-one, Elizabeth got her first adult job. She became a speech therapist at a public school, working with children with special needs. However, by the end of the school year, she became pregnant, and she was replaced by another teacher the next year. She gave birth to a daughter, who was named

The University of Houston, where Elizabeth Warren obtained her college degree

Amelia Louise after her aunt (Bessie Amelia) and mother (Pauline Louise). The Warrens seemed like a typical 1970s nuclear family. Jim went to work, where he earned enough to support his family, and Elizabeth stayed home and looked after home and child—or at least tried to. She sewed, made home repairs, and attempted to cook—an area in which she clearly lacked talent, setting the kitchen on fire several times and giving the family food poisoning twice. Despite her best efforts, being a full-time housewife was clearly not for her. At the same time, she felt guilty for not wanting to stay home with her daughter. She would have liked to return to teaching, but she knew that her husband would object strenuously to her being gone at a full-time job. Instead, she came up with the idea of returning to school. At first, Jim objected, but eventually he gave in. After considering a number of options for graduate school, she decided to study law. One reason was that, on a visit to Oklahoma, she was encouraged by some of the members of her high school debate team to try law school. She claims her decision was influenced by two other factors: the lawyers she saw on TV primarily fought for good people in trouble, and it would be cool for her daughter to be able to tell people her mother was a lawyer. Moreover, getting a law degree would be a serious challenge, which appealed to her. Her mother still hadn't come around to the idea of a woman being anything other than a wife and mother. The women's liberation movement was just becoming a major force in the mid-1970s, and with it came the idea that women should have equality with men. When Elizabeth told her mother she was going to graduate school to become a lawyer, her mother warned her not to become "one of those crazy women's libbers."[8]

Surviving Law School

Every morning, during her three years in law school, Elizabeth would drop Amelia off at daycare, drive to

Rutgers University Law School for classes, and pick her daughter up in the afternoon. Warren thrived in law school. Given her affinity for debating, it's natural that she enjoyed making legal arguments and practicing cross-examination with the other students. In her autobiography, *A Fighting Chance*, she tells of an incident that happened not long after she started law school. In the course of giving an example, a professor referred to "the guy's secretary, a typical dumb blonde." Another woman in the class began to boo. After a moment, the rest of the class joined in, booing and hissing. Warren says, "The professor looked up quickly and then actually staggered back as if he had been hit. One tiny collective action and his world had just shifted a bit. So had mine."[9]

Warren was studying to be a lawyer at a time when women employed in law firms were almost exclusively legal secretaries and clerks. Even many women who had law degrees were offered these jobs when applying to work at law firms. Nonetheless, after her second year of law school, Warren managed to get a summer job interning at a Wall Street law firm. She used the money to buy a second car and get her teeth straightened.

By the time another year had gone by and she was ready to graduate, she was pregnant again. What had seemed a bright future began to slip out of reach. Needless to say, once they saw she was pregnant, none of the firms she applied to offered her a job. Several weeks after graduation, her son Alex was born. She needed a new plan.

CHAPTER TWO

Getting Started

A t twenty-six, with two children to look after, Elizabeth Warren could have just given up. Instead, she decided to take the bar exam, which one must pass to get a license to practice law. With the license in hand, she hung up a sign saying "Elizabeth Warren, Attorney-at-Law" on a lamppost in front of her house and started to practice law out of her home. She handled real estate closings for house sales, small lawsuits, and business incorporations.

Then she got a call one day from her old university, Rutgers. They needed someone to take over teaching a

Elizabeth Warren teaching a law school class. Rutgers gave her the opportunity to teach at the college level.

legal writing class one night a week and asked if she'd be interested. Warren was thrilled to be teaching again, and the next semester she was invited back. Then her husband was transferred back to Houston.

Elizabeth was crushed at the idea of having to give up teaching, but then she thought of applying for a teaching position at the University of Houston law school. She wrote a letter, sent them her résumé, and eventually was hired to teach contract law and run the school's legal writing program. For the first time, she had a job with a future because it was a full-time **"tenure**-track" job, which meant that it could lead to a permanent position. Over time, she added business and finance law courses to her schedule. Besides working, she still had to perform the functions of a mother of two young children—carpooling, making cookies for bake sales, taking a turn as a girl scout leader, and the like. Alex was a problem. One day-care solution after another failed to work out, and finally Warren, at her wit's end, called her aunt Bee. After listening to her niece, Bee got on a plane with her Pekingese and seven suitcases and came to stay and look after the children.

Warren's marriage was not doing as well as her career, however. According to Elizabeth, Jim had a problem with the fact that she was focused on her career rather than on housewifely duties. Elizabeth was nineteen when Jim married her, and at twenty-eight she was a different person—a grown woman and a professional one. Elizabeth and Jim separated in 1979 and divorced the following year. However, Elizabeth retained the last name Warren, for the children's sake.

Warren was now a single mother with two children. She still had Aunt Bee for assistance, but Aunt Bee was elderly now, and more help would be useful. Her parents were still living in Oklahoma. At sixty-seven, her father was still working as a maintenance man, but manual work was getting harder for him. Still, he was determined to keep the job as long as possible because it meant that he and Warren's mother got a free apartment to live in. Warren figured that if they would agree to move to Houston, they, along with Aunt Bee, could look after the children, and Warren could save money on childcare and cover their expenses. Her parents came. Aunt Bee cooked, her mother ran errands, and her father performed repairs.

A New Life

Over the summer, while her family looked after the children, Warren attended a course for professors who wanted to learn about economics. Among the other attendees was an attractive professor, Bruce Mann, who taught law history at the University of Connecticut. Mann had been a tennis instructor, so Warren asked him to give her a tennis lesson. Mann later said she was the worst student he'd ever taught. Mann had both a law degree and a PhD in history. The two hit it off, and in 1980, two years after first meeting, they married. Warren had recently turned thirty-one. She continued to keep the name Warren to make it easier for the children.

Mann quit his job and became a visiting professor at the University of Houston. His job would only last one year, so the two started looking for jobs that would allow them both to teach in the same city. Eventually, they were offered teaching jobs at the University of Texas (UT) at Austin, which had one of the best law schools in the country. The teaching jobs were only a one-year commitment, a chance for the university to evaluate them. Nonetheless, glad to be able to be together, the couple accepted.

They sold the house in Houston, packed up a U-Haul truck, and moved with the children to a rented house in Austin, 160 miles (257 kilometers) from Houston. Warren's parents, who had their own house in Houston, along with Aunt Bee, remained behind, waiting to see if things worked out.

At UT, Warren offered to teach a course in bankruptcy law. Bankruptcy is defined as "a legal proceeding involving a person or business that is unable to repay outstanding debts. The bankruptcy process begins with a petition filed by the debtor, which is most common, or on behalf of creditors, which is less common. All of the debtor's assets are measured and evaluated, and the assets may be used to repay a portion of outstanding debt."[1]

Bankruptcy can be a long and difficult process. This subject would become an area of great interest to Warren because of the effect bankruptcy can have on families. One of the challenges of teaching this subject was that a new bankruptcy law had recently been passed, one that afforded more protection to families filing for bankruptcy. The law was so new that its provisions had yet to be incorporated into the legal textbooks. Warren had to issue copies of the law to the students and conduct the class by discussing specific sections.

When the year was up, UT didn't offer Warren and Mann permanent positions, so they returned to Houston, and Warren once again took up teaching there. A year later, however, UT did offer Warren a permanent position. So, she packed up the children—and this time her parents and Aunt Bee—and the family moved back to Austin. UT did not have a teaching position for Mann. Instead, he was hired by Washington University in St. Louis, 825 miles (1,328 km) from Austin. The couple carried on a long-distance relationship while still trying to find a university that would hire both of them.

Part of being a professor is doing research and publishing articles and/or books. The subject that interested Warren most was bankruptcy. She wanted to know what kind of people declared bankruptcy—and why. On some level, she hoped to find out that these people were cheaters or deadbeats, people who were extravagant and then used bankruptcy as a way to get out of paying their debts. If the people who went bankrupt brought it on themselves, then it couldn't happen to good middle-class people. This was a comforting thought for a woman who had a tremendous fear of being poor because of her early life.

For her foray into research, she found two partners: Terry Sullivan, a young sociologist, and Jay Westbrook, a bankruptcy expert with seven years of legal experience. The three set out to gather data about families who declared bankruptcy. Their approach was different from that of most legal professors of the period, who tended to write articles based on theory rather than perform empirical studies based on analysis of hard data. The bankruptcy research team started by creating a database of information from court cases of people who had filed for bankruptcy protection. Today the process is often carried out electronically or by mail, but in those days, people filing for bankruptcy had to appear before a judge, so Warren went to the San Antonio courthouse to study the people who came to file for bankruptcy. She says, "I expected people in bankruptcy to look scruffy or shifty or generally disreputable. But what struck me was that they looked so *normal* ... I didn't stay long. I felt as if I knew everyone in that courtroom, and I wanted out of there. It was like staring at a car crash, a car crash involving people you knew."[2]

The data collected by the team confirmed Warren's impression at the courthouse—the people who filed for bankruptcy were ordinary middle-class people. The data the researchers obtained from other parts of the country further confirmed what they had found in San Antonio. Most of the people declaring bankruptcy were regular people, often with families. The team found that nearly 90 percent of the people who declared bankruptcy had one of three reasons: a health problem, job loss, or a family breakup due to divorce or the death of a spouse. Their homes were mortgaged, their cars had loans on them, and they had maxed out their credit cards. They declared bankruptcy out of desperation. Moved by what she had learned, Warren took her first steps into the public arena, giving speeches on the subject of bankruptcy. She began to be invited to participate in panels on the subject.

In 1985, Warren and Mann finally both received full-time job offers from the same school, the University of Pennsylvania in Philadelphia. The university hired Warren to teach bankruptcy law and Mann to teach legal history. The university agreed to continue supporting Warren's bankruptcy research. A long-distance relationship is always hard on both parties, and the opportunity for both to work at the same place was appealing, so they accepted. However, the decision meant moving the entire family from

Being a Teacher

From the beginning of her career as a teacher, Warren was demanding of her students. She banned notebook computers in class, and she used a question-and-answer format, which required her students to be prepared even in large lecture-hall settings. She required them to answer questions, even if she had to feed them bits of information until they got the answer. Despite the demands she placed on students, she was admired by them, as well as by the faculty. Students considered her tough but fair, inspiring, and accessible. Warren won student-nominated teaching awards at four of the five universities where she taught. She won Harvard's Sacks-Freund Award twice. Warren loved teaching. Recalling her professor days in an interview, she said:

> I get to watch light bulbs go off ... I can look out in a room and I'm teaching a really hard point and you can see students' faces are like—they look grim. Struggling. And, then, it clicks.[3]

Texas to Pennsylvania. In the end, Warren, Mann, the children, and Aunt Bee, who was now eighty-six, moved. However, Warren's parents decided to return to Oklahoma instead, and they bought a house near two of Warren's brothers.

In addition to teaching college law classes, Elizabeth Warren
performed research on bankruptcy.

Predatory Practices

Because it is such a central issue in Elizabeth Warren's career, understanding bankruptcy and its effects on ordinary people is central to understanding her. Warren first started researching bankruptcy in the wake of the 1980s recession. It wasn't surprising that people went bankrupt when economic times were bad. However, as the years went by, much to her surprise, she found the number of families declaring bankruptcy continued to increase—regardless of whether times were good or bad economically. By 1990, the number of families declaring bankruptcy had doubled from ten years earlier—to seven hundred thousand.

One factor in this trend was increasing interest rates on credit extended to families. Interest is the amount that the bank charges for the use of the money it lends to people. From the founding of the United States until the 1980s, the amount of interest that could be charged for loans was limited by the government. Keeping interest at a reasonable level makes it more certain that people can pay their loans back, which makes the banking system stable. As demonstrated by the economic crisis of 2008, when large numbers of people cannot repay their loans, including mortgages, the banks lose huge amounts of money and risk going out of business. Without banks to provide credit to businesses, businesses fail and people lose their jobs, resulting in more people who can't repay their loans—or pay their bills. This causes even more business to fail, resulting in a downward spiral and producing a recession or even a depression. This is the reason that the **Federal Reserve** acted to stop very large banks from failing in 2008.

In the 1980s, politicians had the idea that **deregulation** would make companies more profitable, and this in turn would improve the economy. The laws regulating interest rates were eliminated, and banks raised fees on credit cards to very high levels—sometimes more than 20 percent. They only collected these fees, however, if people didn't pay off their credit cards, so banks started aiming their promotion of credit cards at people who would only be able to make the minimum payment, rather than the full balance, each month—and who sometimes struggled to do that.

Because she was a professor and not yet involved in politics, Elizabeth Warren had the advantage of being able to find out the bankers' perspective without making them defensive. They were willing to talk frankly to an academic, in a way they would most likely not have talked to someone who worked for the government. In 1990, because of her academic work on bankruptcy, Warren was invited to do a one-day seminar for management at Citibank, which was interested in finding ways to reduce its losses from people filing for bankruptcy. At one point, she suggested to the Citibank executives that, if they wanted to lose less money from bankruptcy filings, they should stop lending money to people who were in financial difficulty already. The response she received was, "We appreciate your presentation ... but we have no interest in cutting back on our lending to these people. They are the ones who provide most of our profits."[4] Instead of practicing fiscally responsible lending, the banks sought to get the government to limit bankruptcy protection. Warren was incensed by the attitude of the banks. In her view, they were entrapping people into debt they could not repay, then denying them protection when a problem arose, such as being laid off or having a medical emergency. However, as a professor, she had no power to affect bank practices.

In 1989, Elizabeth Warren and her fellow researchers, Teresa A. Sullivan and Jay Lawrence Westbrook, wrote a book, *As We Forgive Our Debtors*, which profiled the people who went bankrupt and discussed the law and statistics. The book won the 1990 Silver Gavel Award from the American Bar Association, and it further established Warren's reputation as a bankruptcy expert. In 1992, Warren and Mann were both invited to teach for a year at the Harvard University Law School. At the end of the year, Warren was offered a permanent position, but the university didn't have a spot for her husband. Unwilling to engage in a long-distance relationship again, Warren turned the job down. Back at the University of Pennsylvania, she continued to give speeches about bankruptcy. She wrote articles and started a book. However, the Harvard dean periodically renewed the offer. By this time, she was forty-five and her children were grown. Mann insisted that if Warren really wanted to make a difference, she should take the job at Harvard. It would give her a much more prestigious platform from which to speak. Eventually, Mann was also offered a full-time job on the Harvard faculty. He still works there.

CHAPTER THREE

Taking on the Banks

I n 1995, President Bill Clinton appointed Congressman Mike Synar to head the newly created National Bankruptcy Review Commission. Congressman Synar knew Warren from their high school days and invited her to join the commission. Synar convinced Warren that by joining the commission she could help the families she had become concerned about in the course of her research. Since the commission was a part-time job, she continued to teach at Harvard University, commuting periodically to Washington, DC. She managed research for the commission and wrote drafts of proposals. The commission's job was to make recommendations to

Congressman Mike Synar, head of President Clinton's National Bankruptcy Review Commission

Congress for changes in the bankruptcy law. Members represented different parties and viewpoints. For example, whereas Warren was concerned about families who suffered from bankruptcy, another member of the commission, Judge Judy Jones, was concerned that lenient bankruptcy laws would encourage people to run up debts and then use bankruptcy to avoid having to pay them. After two years of work and hard-fought internal battles, the commission produced a report for Congress. The report recommended making only minor changes to the law, rather than eliminating protections for families filing for bankruptcy, as the banking industry wanted.

The People vs. the Banks

Unable to influence the commission to make the changes it wanted in the bankruptcy law, the banking industry lobbied members of Congress directly. Together with congressmen who supported their position, they drafted their own bankruptcy bill and presented it to Congress before the commission could finalize theirs. By getting their bill to the floor first, they made it harder for the commission's bill to win support. The bank-backed bill didn't eliminate bankruptcy protections, but it did add a lot of complex changes that would make it harder for people to discharge their debts. Warren went back to teaching and research, but unable to abandon the fight, she also continued to give speeches about bankruptcy. One of her speeches was heard by Ted Kennedy's chief counsel, who arranged a meeting

with the Massachusetts senator. Warren convinced Senator Kennedy to lead a fight against the bill in the Senate. In 1998, Warren met with First Lady Hillary Clinton and obtained her support. Despite the efforts of Ted Kennedy and other members of Congress who joined the cause, the banking industry's version of the bill passed the House and Senate and was sent to President Clinton. President Clinton, encouraged by Hillary, vetoed the bill.

The banking industry didn't give up; they resubmitted the bill in 2002. This time George W. Bush was president, and he stated that he would sign it if it passed. However, Senators Ted Kennedy and Dick Durbin of Illinois succeeded in adding amendments to the bill that made it unpalatable to members of the House, which killed the bill without a vote. Looking back, despite the difficulties of working on the commission and trying to block the banking industry bill, Elizabeth Warren feels that the process enriched her understanding:

The work would have been so sterile [in academia] by comparison with what it turned out to be. Oh, yeah, I'd have had great ideas for how 11-USC-1326-B-2II [a bankruptcy statute] should be modified in order to achieve a more harmonious result, but oddly enough, it was wading into the politics and beginning to understand the rest of this world that is what shapes law. It's a law and society point. The political part ultimately enriched my understanding of the scope of the problems. It took me far beyond bankruptcy and much more into questions about what's happening to the middle class.[1]

The Two-Income Trap

In 2001, Warren and her daughter, Amelia, then thirty years old, decided to collaborate on a book, *The Two-Income Trap*. The book compared the plight of middle-class families in 1971, when Warren was a young mother, and those in the early 2000s, when her daughter was one. Wages for middle-class jobs had stopped growing in the period from the 1970s to the 2000s, but costs, such as housing prices, continued to rise. More and more women were forced to enter the workforce so the family could cover all its expenses. The "two-income trap" meant that as two-income households became the norm, prices rose to levels that were barely affordable by two-income families. Meanwhile, single-earner families found it even more difficult to make ends meet. Eventually, inflation in prices meant that even two-income middle-class families could not save money for emergencies such as a health issue or losing a job. Families with no other resources turned to credit, especially credit cards, and if disaster hit, they couldn't pay the debt back. When the book appeared in print, its content was covered by newspapers and magazines, and Elizabeth Warren was invited to appear on NPR (National Public Radio), CNN, and the *Today* show. This national attention inspired her to try to reach out to the presidential candidates in 2004, including John Edwards and John Kerry. They were impressed by *The Two-Income Trap*, and she had supportive meetings with them. She also attempted to arrange a

meeting with President George W. Bush, but she got no response from the White House.

As a result of the book, Warren had the opportunity to go on the *Dr. Phil* show. This gave her the chance to warn viewers about the dangers of taking on debt, but more important was the feedback on the book from Dr. Phil after the show. He liked the book but thought it was too academic for the general public. He suggested that she write a book for a mainstream audience. She and Amelia took his advice, and in 2003, they started work on *All Your Worth*. It provided readers with information on how to handle their finances to ensure a secure economic future.

In 2005, Congress finally passed a bill backed by the banking industry. It made the process of filing for bankruptcy protection more complicated and more expensive. For a decade, Warren and her political allies had held off the banking industry, but in the end, the banks won. The effect on Warren was lasting. She says, "The bankruptcy wars changed me forever. Even before this grinding battle, I had begun to understand the terrible squeeze on the middle class. But it was this fight that showed me how badly the playing field was tilted and taught me the squeeze wasn't accidental."[2]

The Crash of 2008

Warren continued to advocate for families facing bankruptcy. In 2008, the banks' practices finally caught up with them. They had given mortgages to a vast

After the 2008 housing crash and subsequent economic crisis, many middle-class people lost their jobs and their homes.

number of people with high-risk credit ratings, enticing them to take on debts whose complicated terms they did not understand. There were often challenging provisions, such as payments that increased over time. People who were unfamiliar with this type of finance would discover, after signing the mortgage papers, they were responsible for thousands of dollars more annually than they had been led to believe they would owe. In other cases, banks quoted payments that looked very low because they didn't cover property taxes and mandatory property insurance, which are normally included in a mortgage payment.

At the same time, banks created and marketed a new investment product, credit default swaps (CDSs), which

allowed purchasers to invest in a pool of mortgages, many of which were not financially sound (although investors were led to believe all the debt in the pool was sound by brokers selling the CDSs). CDSs gave banks the ability to issue mortgages to people with poor credit, who were unlikely to be able to make their payments, and then offload the risk onto investors and make money from both the mortgagees and the investors. In 2008, large numbers of these families with high-risk credit ratings were unable to pay their mortgages. The banks found themselves faced with vast losses from people who couldn't repay their loans, all at the same time. Normally, when people can't pay their mortgage, the bank takes the house back and sells it. However, so many people defaulted at once that there were mass **foreclosures**, putting a glut of houses on the market. The price for houses fell **precipitously**. Now the property held by the bank was worth much less than the amount of money they had lent out. In some cases, the losses were so many and so great that there was the danger of banks failing. Moreover, as housing prices fell, many people found that they were making payments on houses that were now worth significantly less than what they owed. The effects of these bank losses reverberated throughout the economy, resulting in the worst recession since the Great Depression of the 1930s. The government stepped in, taking steps to keep the failure of giant banks from causing a second Great Depression. Congress authorized $700 billion for the US Treasury to provide to banks to keep them solvent, under a program called the **Troubled Assets Relief Program (TARP)**. Distributing the money to banks to shore them up was the responsibility of the Treasury. In return, the Treasury would get assets from the banks, which it would sell at a later date for repayment.

Senate Majority Leader Harry Reid called Elizabeth Warren and asked her to come to Washington and help oversee the US Treasury's handling of the government bailout of the banks. Warren agreed to join the five-person Congressional Oversight Panel (COP), whose job was to ascertain what the Treasury was doing with the money and write reports to Congress. Neither getting information out of the Treasury nor working with the other members of the panel was easy. Eventually, the panel discovered that the assets the Treasury was accepting in return for funds were consistently worth less than the amount of money the banks were receiving from the Treasury. In short, the Treasury was subsidizing the banks. Eventually the value of the assets did increase to the point where the government got its money back, but there was no way to know that would happen. At the time, it was another example of the banks being supported at the people's expense, and Warren was appalled.

The longer she worked on the panel, the more aware Warren became that the plight of the people who lost their homes was completely irrelevant to the Treasury Department. Their programs were strictly designed to rescue the banks. Saving the banks was important, of course.

Elizabeth Warren worked with the Congressional Oversight Panel (COP) to monitor the activities of the Treasury Department during the 2009 bank bailout.

If the major banks failed, then businesses that depended on them would fail, and people would lose their homes anyway. However, there was no aspect of the Treasury's programs that did anything to help the flood of people who were losing their homes, and this incensed Warren.

Because the commission involved both Republicans and Democrats, the viewpoints of the participants often diverged. Warren has stated that her experience on the commission taught her something valuable about **bipartisanship** (when members of two different parties work together): the result doesn't have to be the "lowest common denominator"—the simplest, least controversial

The Outsiders

In May 2010, *Time* magazine ran an article titled "The New Sheriffs of Wall Street." The article profiled three women: Elizabeth Warren; Sheila Bair, chair of the Federal Deposit Insurance Corporation, which insures deposits in banks; and Mary Schapiro, chair of the Securities and Exchange Commission (SEC), which oversees the firms that trade stocks. The tagline of the article states:

> They skipped the partner track. They were underestimated by men. But the women who will regulate banking and finance for the next generation—Mary Schapiro, Sheila Bair and Elizabeth Warren—are not accustomed to taking no for an answer.[3]

The article goes on to say that these women, who were Wall Street outsiders, made their careers by "outhustling" the men around them. They were willing to challenge the status quo, and they were the ones who would protect the consumers of the next generation.

Elizabeth Warren felt that being an outsider gave her a unique perspective on the financial system. She had nothing invested in the system, so she could question everything. Warren stayed with the Congressional Oversight Panel until September 2010. She was frustrated by many of the situations she encountered, but she had some important victories. In her book *A Fighting Chance*, she points out some of these:

- Their July 2009 report pointed out that the bonuses that had been paid to the heads of banks were

Elizabeth Warren was featured in a 2010 *Time* magazine article.

owed to taxpayers. The report helped the Treasury reclaim billions of dollars.

- They made sure that the government bailout of the auto industry, which saved 1.1 million jobs, was in accordance with law and economic policy.

- They revealed information about how the regulatory system contributed to the economic crisis because the system was too underfunded and the regulators too cozy with the bankers. This provided ammunition to those who would later try to reform the regulatory system.

statement that both parties can agree on. The members of the commission often argued. The process was hard, but compromise resulted in reports that were strong and meaningful. This experience would serve Warren well later in her career, when she became a senator and had to work with members of the other party.

Neil Barsofsky, who was in charge of TARP oversight at the Treasury, says of Elizabeth Warren, "[The] Treasury's descriptions of what was happening were very skewed towards the positive and often incomprehensible. There was this reluctance towards transparency … [and Warren] helped bring light in a lot of dark areas."[4] While the Treasury played ball with the banks, not requiring them to explain what they were doing with the billions in TARP bailout money, Elizabeth Warren worked both directly and through the media, criticizing the government's secrecy and the fact that, after the bailout, the banks had escaped punishment. One bank vice-chairman is quoted as saying that on Wall Street, Warren is regarded as "the Devil incarnate."[5]

Warren says of her time on the panel:

Our oversight of the bailout wasn't perfect, not by any stretch. But I saw what was possible. We took an obscure little panel that could have disappeared without a trace and worked hard to become the eyes and ears and voice for a lot of people who had been cut out [by] the system. And every now and again we landed a blow for the people who were getting pounded by the economic crash. That felt good. It felt really good.[6]

While she was working for the Congressional Oversight Panel, Warren came up with another idea. From speaking to large numbers of people in financial trouble, she learned that many of them had been deceived by credit card companies, finance companies, and other businesses that provide financing for large purchases, such as cars. These companies often engaged in practices such as quoting one interest rate to a borrower and then later raising it to a much higher rate. How could they do this? Somewhere in the pages of fine print for the financing contract was a statement that allowed them to do so. For instance, the contract might say that the quoted rate was a preliminary rate only good for a short period of time; after that time, the company could raise the rate significantly. If the purchaser didn't read all the fine print or didn't understand the terminology used in the contract—well, that was their problem. Warren's solution was to create an agency to make rules governing such contracts and to require the industry to put the terms in plain English. This would apply to all types of consumer credit: credit cards, mortgages, student loans, payday loans, and the like.

Protecting Consumers

In 2007, Warren wrote an article in *Democracy* magazine explaining her idea for a consumer financial protection bureau, but the idea didn't catch fire until after the stock market crash of 2008. In 2009, Congress was seeking ways to increase the regulation of the banking industry, whose shoddy lending practices had resulted in millions of foreclosures and crashed the financial system. While Warren was working on the Congressional Oversight Panel, overseeing the TARP program, Damon Silvers, general consul of the AFL-CIO, a major labor union, invited her to attend a meeting on financial reform. The meeting was held at the Washington headquarters of the AFL-CIO. Attendees consisted of members of nonprofit agencies and advocacy groups who wanted to protect the rights of working families. They represented civil rights organizations, consumer groups, religious organizations, and labor unions. They anticipated that the banking industry would throw its considerable resources—and its lobbyists—into an effort to limit regulation.

At the meeting, Warren presented her idea for a consumer financial protection agency. There were laws governing credit cards and loans, but the enforcement of those laws was distributed across seven different federal agencies. Further, all of them had other primary responsibilities. The method by which regulators were chosen for particular banks made matters worse. There were two banking regulators. Their budgets depended on how many banks they signed up. Therefore, it was in their interest to be friendly to the bankers they met with. This naturally undermined the process of oversight. In addition, the landscape of lending is continually changing over time. New types of lenders had appeared that were not in the regulations that covered banks. Among these were:

- Payday lenders: These are companies that provide short-term loans to people, often with inflated interest rates, to tide them over until payday, hence the designation.

- Title lenders: These companies lend money to a person who, in turn, surrenders the title to his or her car. If the loan isn't paid back, the lender can sell the car.

- Mortgage companies: Like banks, mortgage companies provide mortgages, but because they are not banks, they are not subject to banking regulations.

All of these lenders fell outside the existing regulatory framework, leaving consumers open to predatory practices.

Warren's vision was for the government to create a new agency, whose purpose was to oversee and regulate consumer lending. It would have responsibility for writing regulations for all types of credit used by ordinary people, such as credit cards, mortgages, payday lending, car loans, and student loans. Further, it would be able to write new regulations as regulatory practices changed. Achieving this goal would embroil Elizabeth Warren in a new series of battles.

CHAPTER FOUR

Protecting the People

O ne of Elizabeth Warren's major accomplishments in Washington, DC, was the establishment of the Consumer Financial Protection Bureau (CFPB). The agency would be able to write regulations that would require banks and other lenders to disclose previously hidden terms. It would also be able to create regulations allowing consumers to remedy situations in which they were treated unfairly. Warren's entire professional career had been devoted to fighting for the rights of ordinary people who were struggling financially. However, the CFPB would take her efforts to a new level. Given that creating a new

President Barack Obama signs the document to create the Consumer Financial Protection Bureau.

agency required the support of Congress and the president of the United States, her success in getting the agency established is even more impressive.

Fighting for the CFPB

Warren knew that establishing the CFPB would not be easy. Her efforts would be opposed by the huge banks and their lobbyists, and she knew from past experience that she could not expect much cooperation from politicians who relied on campaign contributions from big businesses.

To garner support for the idea, she pitched it to the general public. She equated the new CFPB with earlier federal agencies and the good they had done for the public. For example, the creation of the Consumer Product Safety Commission had resulted in the establishment of safety standards for consumer goods and the recall of unsafe products. Warren emphasized that Congress cannot pass a law to control every individual product, but an agency has the flexibility to apply similar standards across a wide range of products, including new ones as they are introduced. The agency would require that the terms of contracts be spelled out in clear language that consumers could understand. It would try to eliminate deceptive practices, such as advertising a 5 percent interest rate and using the fine print to hide the fact that it would change to 25 percent at a later date.

In her book *A Fighting Chance*, Warren states that she repeatedly heard the same arguments against the creation of such an agency. The following is a summary of some of the objections and her responses:

- *The agency would fix prices.* The agency wouldn't set prices, just make the real prices clearer.

- *The agency would enlarge the nanny state* (a government that treats its citizens like children) *by controlling people's use of credit.* The agency wouldn't keep people from relying too much on credit; it would just make the costs clear.

- *The agency would stop innovation by preventing the creation of new financial products.* The agency wouldn't stop banks from creating new products; it would just require their terms and costs to be clear.

- *The agency would put banks out of business.* This would happen only if a bank was relying on deception to trick consumers. Honest banks would have a more level playing field.

Warren won the support of senators such as Ted Kennedy of Massachusetts, Dick Durbin of Illinois, and Chuck Schumer of New York. They agreed to introduce in the Senate a bill to create the agency. She also had the support of Congressman Brad Miller of North Carolina in the House of Representatives.

At the same time that the bill for the new agency was being introduced in Congress, Congressman Barney Frank and Senator Chris Dodd were working on a

Congressman Barney Frank drafted the Dodd-Frank financial services reform bill along with Senator Chris Dodd.

financial reform bill that would cover a variety of areas. It was 2009, and after the 2008 financial crisis, it was apparent that the financial system needed reforming. Elizabeth Warren met with Congressman Frank, who was then head of the House Financial Services Committee. The congressman was juggling a vast number of elements that affected the financial system, and Warren knew the agency wouldn't be a priority. Her pitch to the congressman was straightforward: Supporting the agency could help win support from the public for the rest of his bill because it dealt with something they could understand. Most ordinary people don't know what a financial derivative is, but they do know what hidden interest rate increases on a credit card or mortgage are. She succeeded in getting Frank to include the new agency in the financial reform package.

In June 2009, Warren discovered that she also had the support of President Barack Obama. She received an invitation to hear President Obama announce the details of a financial reform package. Attendees at the announcement were given copies of a document that described the various elements incorporated into the reform package. She saw that the creation of the Consumer Financial Protection Bureau was included.

Congressman Frank and Senator Dodd fought to push the financial reform bill through Congress. Meanwhile, Elizabeth Warren went into full gear. She called reporters and wrote editorial pieces for newspapers in support of the new agency. She spent hours and hours contacting individual members of Congress to convince them to vote in favor of creating the agency. The banks' lobbyists were also competing for the representatives' attention. In September 2009, Warren returned to teaching at Harvard and continued her work on the commission that oversaw TARP. Nonetheless, she kept fighting for the Consumer Financial Protection Bureau. In December 2009, the financial reform bill passed in the House of Representatives. In the Senate, it ran into more opposition.

In January 2010, Elizabeth Warren heard that Senator Dodd was going to give up the CFPB in return for acceptance of other provisions. It would be several weeks before the Senate Banking Committee sent a final version of the bill to the Senate floor for a vote. That gave Warren time to fight for the CFPB's inclusion. She went on a media blitz, appearing on talk shows and trying to get the word out through as many media outlets as possible. She wasn't willing to compromise on quality to get the agency approved, however. Warren was asked by the *Huffington Post* if she would accept a watered-down version of the agency. In *A Fighting Chance*, she recounts her response:

> *I said no. "My first choice is a strong consumer agency. My second choice is no agency at all and plenty of blood and teeth left on the floor ... My 99th choice is some mouthful of mush that doesn't get the job done." I said that we should either stand and fight for something worthwhile or go get honest work somewhere else. I wanted nothing to do with a watchdog that could do nothing but whimper.*[1]

Designing an Agency

President Obama signed the Dodd-Frank bill into law on July 21, 2010. It included the creation of the Consumer Financial Protection Bureau and gave President Obama the authority to appoint an independent director of the agency for a five-year term, subject to confirmation by the Senate. The director would have broad authority to write and enforce rules governing credit cards, mortgages, and other loans.

The president invited Elizabeth Warren to accept a temporary position working for Secretary of the Treasury Timothy Geithner to set up the agency. Ultimately, President Obama appointed her to not one but two jobs. She was given the positions of "Special Advisor to the Secretary of the Treasury on the Consumer Financial Protection Bureau" and "Assistant to the President." The latter designation made it clear that her work had the president's backing.

Warren's new jobs required her full-time attention. She resigned from the COP and took a leave of absence from Harvard. She moved to Washington, while her husband continued to teach, commuting to visit her each week. Warren immediately started working on various aspects of the new agency. She and her staff set up a consumer hotline to field complaints, created a financial literacy department to educate consumers, put up a website, and started writing regulations.

President Obama was now tasked with appointing a director for the agency. Elizabeth Warren was one possible choice. However, the president was faced with a dilemma. If he didn't select her, he risked angering his liberal supporters, who felt that she was the logical choice. If he did choose her, however, he risked turning the financial industry further against him and the Democratic Party. Warren's appointment would also start a fight with Republicans over her confirmation.

According to an August 2010 article in the *Washington Post*, Elizabeth Warren provoked wildly different reactions

How the Consumer Protection Bureau Helps People

According to a 2014 *Mother Jones* article, Elizabeth Warren's CFPB, then three years old, had already achieved ten important accomplishments:

1. Mortgage lenders were no longer able to deceive consumers into accepting a high-priced loan even if they qualified for a lower-interest loan.

2. Lenders could no longer give mortgages to borrowers without verifying their ability to pay. This reduced the number of foreclosures.

3. Lenders were forced to make a serious effort to help borrowers avoid foreclosure before foreclosing on a property.

4. The CFPB required most mortgage lenders to give applicants a list of free or low-cost housing counselors. These advisors can verify that the borrowers are not being taken advantage of.

5. Lenders selling high-cost mortgages were required to have the property's value determined by an independent appraiser.

6. Debt collectors, such as payday lenders, were subjected to regulation. Those who engaged in predatory practices were identified and disciplined.

7. Credit card companies that engaged in illegal practices, such as misleading credit card offers, excessive late fees, or charging people for services they didn't sign up for, were forced to pay refunds to affected people.

8. Nonbank student loan lenders were being monitored to make sure they complied with fair lending laws.

9. The CFPB was making sure that military service people weren't charged excessive fees by those providing military lending services.

10. The CFPB had set up a consumer help center whose sole job was to assist consumers in fixing their problems with banks and lenders.[2]

As Elizabeth Warren envisioned, the CFPB was making a difference in ordinary people's lives and helping them combat unfair practices by the banking industry.

President Obama announces the appointment of Elizabeth Warren as a special advisor to help set up the new Consumer Financial Protection Bureau.

from different groups: "She's either the plain-spoken, supremely smart crusader for middle-class families that her supporters adore, or she's the power-hungry headline seeker her critics loathe." The article goes on to say, "But no one disputes that she's the most prominent and polarizing candidate to lead the new Bureau of Consumer Financial Protection … The bureau's director will be the most powerful new banking regulator in decades and the first with the exclusive mission of focusing on consumers."[3]

The Obama administration considered several potential choices for the job aside from Elizabeth Warren. Among these were Assistant Treasury Secretary Michael S. Barr and Deputy Assistant Attorney General Eugene Kimmelman from the Justice Department's Antitrust Division. Warren received enthusiastic support from consumer groups, labor unions, and many Democratic members of Congress. The financial industry was adamantly against her appointment. Anton Schutz, president of the investment firm Mendon Capital Advisors, was quoted by the Reuters news service as saying, "I get disgusted every time I hear her speak. It's like she's sitting in some ivory tower, not understanding the ramifications of anything she says ... Any person you put in that role really ought to have some industry experience."[4] The last statement suggests that the person chosen should be willing to play ball with the companies in the financial industry.

Warren's daughter, Amelia, on the subject of her mother's potential appointment, said, "This is a once-in-a-lifetime moment to do the thing she cares about most ... If she didn't think she could make a difference in Washington right now, she wouldn't be there."[5] A large number of consumer groups, the AFL-CIO labor union, eighty-nine congressmen, and many individuals signed petitions and sent them to the White House, asking President Obama to put Warren in charge of the CFPB. Newspapers and bloggers around the country editorialized in her favor.

Letting Go

Elizabeth Warren had spent months setting up the new agency, ensuring that it would be strong. In the time she spent setting up the agency, she came to love the job and the difference the agency was making in people's lives. She wanted to be the director and to ensure the success of the agency, but the president had made it clear all along that this would be impractical. The Republicans would never confirm her. In the end, President Obama appointed Richard Cordray, whom Warren had hired to run the CFPB's enforcement division. He was the former attorney general of Ohio and had a reputation as a consumer advocate.

Many people blamed Treasury Secretary Timothy Geithner for the president's decision not to appoint Warren to head the CFPB. It was well known that she and Geithner clashed repeatedly when she was performing oversight of the TARP program. Geithner has said that Warren ran her bailout oversight hearings "like made-for-YouTube inquisitions."[6] Geithner, however, denies he was responsible. Instead, he claims that she was passed over because the Senate leadership told the president that it was unlikely the Senate would vote to approve her appointment. According to Geithner:

> The President was torn. Progressives were turning Warren into another whose-side-are-you-on litmus test. The head of the National Organization for Women publicly accused me of blocking Warren, calling me a classic Wall Street sexist. Valerie Jarrett, the President's confidante from Chicago, was pushing hard for Warren, too, and she was worried I would stand in the way. At a meeting with Rahm [Emmanuel, President Obama's chief of staff] and Valerie, I told the

group that if the President wanted to appoint Warren to run the CFPB, I wouldn't try to talk him out of it, but everyone in the room knew she had no chance of being confirmed. The president, who almost never called me at home, made an exception on this issue. It was really eating away at him. He had a huge amount of respect for Warren, but he didn't want an endless confirmation fight, and he was hesitant to nominate someone so divisive that it would undermine the agency's ability to get up and running, as well as its ability to build broader legitimacy beyond the left.[7]

Warren herself says that the president invited her to the White House and told her that the Republicans in the Senate would block attempts to confirm her. She just worried them and the bankers too much.

Although she was not chosen to head the agency she had conceived of, championed, and pushed Congress to approve, in the course of advocating for the bureau, she had gained national attention. She had traveled the country to garner support for the CFPB, appearing on national programs such as *Real Time with Bill Maher* and *The Daily Show with Jon Stewart*, as well as programs on CNBC. This media exposure transformed her into a national figure. She had become of a figure with a reputation for fighting for consumer rights. In her final meeting with the president, he discussed the Senate race in Massachusetts, where Republican Scott Brown was running. He suggested that, if she ran and won, she'd have a great opportunity to fight for the economic issues she cared about.

CHAPTER FIVE

The National Stage

As a result of her work in Washington, Elizabeth Warren began to receive national recognition. In 2009, she was named Bostonian of the Year by the *Boston Globe*, and the Women's Bar Association of Massachusetts presented her with the Lelia J. Robinson Award. The award is named after the first woman who was admitted to the Massachusetts bar and

Elizabeth Warren accepts the Lelia J. Robinson Award from the Women's Bar Association of Massachusetts.

allowed to practice law, in 1882. It is given to a woman who has done pioneering work in law and made a difference in her community.

Time magazine three times included Warren on its list of America's one hundred most influential people—in 2009, 2010, and 2015. The *National Law Journal* has listed Warren as one of the fifty most influential women attorneys in America several times, and in 2010, it recognized her as one of the forty most influential attorneys of the decade. Warren was inducted into the Oklahoma Hall of Fame in 2011. The hall of fame honors residents, or former residents, who perform outstanding service to humanity, Oklahoma, and the United States, and who are known for their public service throughout the state.[1]

Also in 2011, Warren was selected to deliver the commencement address at the Rutgers School of Law–Newark. While there, she was presented with an honorary doctor of laws degree and was granted membership in the Order of the Coif, a prestigious legal honor society. (The "coif" was a round white piece of cloth worn on the wigs of medieval sergeants-at-law, the highest level of lawyer.) In January 2012, the British *New Statesman* magazine identified Warren as one of the top-twenty US progressives.

A Chance to Run

The greatest acknowledgment of Warren's contributions came in 2012, when she made the decision to run for the

US Senate seat left vacant by the death of Ted Kennedy. As with everything else Warren had done in her career, she had to overcome great odds and opposition to achieve this goal. Scott Brown had taken over the Senate seat in a special election after Kennedy died in August 2009, and he finished Kennedy's term, which meant he was up for reelection in November 2012.

In August 2011, Warren got a call from a Democratic Party official, who encouraged her to run for the seat. At the same time, he noted that she probably wouldn't win—he felt that nobody could beat Scott Brown, a Massachusetts native, a moderate Republican, and an ex–state legislator. Brown had high approval ratings, and he was liked by Wall Street, which meant he was well funded.

Warren had reservations about making a run against Brown. Among other issues was the fact that she wasn't born in Massachusetts—or even New England. Despite her lower-middle-class background, she was known as a Harvard professor, which didn't exactly make her seem like a woman of the people. She had no experience running for office—or raising money to do so. She was also sixty-two years old and tired of Washington politics. She knew the way political campaigns were conducted and was aware that her opponents would do their best to find material that would embarrass her. Members of her family could be hurt. Furthermore, no woman had ever been elected senator or governor in Massachusetts.

Scott Brown, Elizabeth Warren's Republican opponent in the 2012 Massachusetts Senate race, speaks at a campaign rally.

Warren started meeting with small groups of voters around the state to see what they thought. On the basis of those meetings, she concluded that people were depending on her to keep fighting for them. In her book *A Fighting Chance*, she describes how a video made at one of the home meetings she attended got national attention. When one of the attendees asked her about the federal budget deficit, she responded:

There is nobody in this country who got rich on his own. Nobody. You built a factory out there? Good for you. But I want to be clear: You moved your goods to market on the roads the rest of us paid for. You hired workers the rest of us paid to educate. You were safe in your factory because of police forces and fire forces that the rest of us paid for. You didn't have to worry that marauding bands would come and seize everything at your factory, and hire someone to protect against this, because of the work the rest of us did. Now look, you built a factory and it turned into something terrific, or a great idea? God bless! Keep a big hunk of it. But part of the underlying social contract is you take a hunk of that and pay forward for the next kid who comes along.[2]

Someone at the meeting filmed her statement and posted it on YouTube. The video clip went viral. It attracted attention from both the left- and right-wing media. Ultra-conservative talk show host Rush Limbaugh accused Warren of being a Marxist. Scott Brown appealed to his banker and Wall Street supporters for funds to defeat her. Warren did her own fundraising and gained over $42 million in donations. Much of this money came from individual donations, including a large amount raised over the internet.

The Native American Controversy

Then came a **brouhaha** about Warren's heritage. Warren's mother had grown up in Indian Territory, before the area became the state of Oklahoma, and she had often talked about the fact that both her parents had some Native American blood. Sixteen years before Warren ran for the Senate, a Harvard official had used the fact that Warren was part Native American to defend the university against charges of a lack of diversity in an article. During the campaign, a reporter uncovered this fact and asked Warren for details of her Native American ancestry. Warren didn't remember the article, and her response failed to satisfy the reporter. This set off a media firestorm by Republicans, who demanded proof of her ancestry and claimed she'd gotten her job at Harvard because she applied as a member of a minority. She didn't have any documentation because her mother's family had never registered for a tribal affiliation. In her grandparents' day, many people in the area didn't bother to register. Warren had learned of her ancestry from the stories her mother told her, and she had mentioned being part Native American in her high school yearbook. Harvard and all the firms that had employed Warren denied that her ethnicity had anything to do with their hiring her. They insisted she had been hired because of her credentials and her competence.

Eventually the controversy died down, and Warren's campaign team set up offices all over the state to contact potential voters. In June, the Democratic Party held its state convention. At that point the race for the Democratic nomination was down to two candidates, Warren and Marisa DeFranco, an immigration lawyer.

During the 2016 presidential campaign, Elizabeth Warren delivered the keynote address at the Democratic National Convention.

Unless 85 percent of the delegates at the convention voted for one of them, the Democratic nominee would be chosen at the polls in the September primary. After both candidates delivered a fifteen-minute speech on why they should be nominated, the delegates voted, and Warren received more than 85 percent of the vote. This was the first time anyone could recall that a candidate had done so in a contested election. Warren was off and running. Her campaign slogan: "The best senator money can't buy."

On the National Stage

In September she attended the Democratic National Convention in Charlotte, North Carolina. Warren had been invited to speak on Wednesday night just before

Bill Clinton gave his address. It was the first time Warren had attended a national convention. She would speak to a live audience of around twenty thousand people and a TV audience of about twenty-five million. When the time came, she spoke about a topic dear to her heart: how the system was rigged, and how middle-class people were being hurt by it. The following are some of the key points from her speech:

I'm here tonight to talk about hard-working people: people who get up early, stay up late, cook dinner and help out with homework; people who can be counted on to help their kids, their parents, their neighbors, and the lady down the street whose car broke down; people who work their hearts out but are up against a hard truth—the game is rigged against them ... People feel like the system is rigged against them. And here's the painful part: they're right. The system is rigged ... The Republican vision is clear: "I've got mine, the rest of you are on your own." Republicans say they don't believe in government. Sure they do. They believe in government to help themselves and their powerful friends. After all, [Republican presidential candidate] Mitt Romney's the guy who said corporations are people. No, Governor Romney, corporations are not people. People have hearts, they have kids, they get jobs, they get sick, they cry, they dance. They live, they love, and they die. And that matters. That matters because we don't run this country for corporations, we run it for people.[3]

The speech Warren delivered incorporated not only the topics she cared about but also the passion with which she approached them. The *Washington Post* had this to say about Warren's speech:

> *We struggled with where to fit the Massachusetts Democratic Senate nominee in our winners and losers post ... The reaction to Warren in the room made clear that if she winds up in the Senate in 2013, she will immediately become part of the 2016 Democratic presidential conversation. But, the heat with which Warren delivered her speech made us wonder that it might not make it slightly harder for her to get to the Senate this fall. Do conservative Democrats and independents in Massachusetts react to that sort of tenor and tone?*[4]

The battle was hard, with the Republicans running negative ads against her and three debates to navigate. For most of the race, Brown was the favorite to win. The weekend before the election, Warren campaign volunteers made seven hundred thousand phone calls and knocked on three hundred thousand doors. Months earlier, when she started her run, victory had seemed impossible, but the people of Massachusetts awarded her the victory. She won by a large margin: 54 to 46 percent of the vote in the highest-turnout election ever held in Massachusetts (73 percent of registered voters). Her victory was historic—she was the first woman to be elected senator from Massachusetts.

On May 8, 2013, Warren introduced her first bill in the US Senate, the Bank on Students Loan Fairness Act. It would require the Federal Reserve (the US federal bank) to lend money to college students at the same rate they lend it to banks. In her first four years in office, she sponsored thirty-seven bills. Among them were the Equal Employment for All Act, the Schedules That Work Act, the Trade Transparency Act, and the Fed Accountability Act. Though the bills she's sponsored have not become law, she has continued to fight on behalf of low-wage workers and to champion women's rights, fair trade, and affordable education.

When Senator John Kerry of Massachusetts resigned his Senate seat to become secretary of state, Warren became the senior senator from Massachusetts, after serving only one month in the Senate. (Each state has a senior and a junior senator.) The designation is more than cosmetic. Traditionally, senior senators get first choice of committees to serve on and make federal appointments in their states.

In the Senate, Warren has been a member of some significant congressional committees. During the 2015–2016 session of Congress, she sat on four subcommittees of the Banking, Housing, and Urban Affairs Committee: the Subcommittee on Economic Policy, the Subcommittee on Housing, Transportation,

In her role as senator, Elizabeth Warren continues to work to better the lives of middle-class people.

and Community Development, the Subcommittee on Financial Institutions and Consumer Protection, and the Subcommittee on Securities, Insurance, and Investment. She also was a member of the Subcommittee on Primary Health and Retirement Security, and the Subcommittee on Children and Families, which are both part of the Committee on Health, Education, Labor, and Pensions. Additionally, she served on the Special Committee on Aging, as well as three subcommittees of the Committee on Energy and Natural Resources.

As a senator, Warren has continued to ask tough questions and demand accountability. This is how Noam Scheiber described her first banking committee meeting, in an article in *New Republic* magazine:

*"Tell me a little bit about the last few times you've taken the biggest financial institutions on Wall Street all the way to a trial," she asked a table full of bank regulators ... An awkward pause ensued, at which point Warren flared her eyes and thrust her head forward, as if to say, "Yes, this is really happening." Until that instant, the regulators believed the world worked one way; suddenly, it was working another. One winced hemorrhoidally as he searched for a place to fix his gaze. The head of an agency called the Office of the Comptroller of the Currency (OCC) appeared to whimper before allowing that the threat of trial was unnecessary for keeping the banks in check— about as **counterfactual** a notion as the industry has ever produced. A third regulator chimed in **affirmatively**. For a few minutes, Warren looked like the only sane person in a mental ward. A video of the exchange has been viewed online more than a million times.*[5]

The 2016 Presidential Campaign

In 2016, Elizabeth Warren's national reputation had reached the point where she was considered a possible candidate for the presidential race. She is certainly the type of candidate who has **populist** appeal for angry voters who feel they have been left out of the economic recovery after the 2008 crash. Warren, however, insisted from the beginning that she was not going to run, and she stuck by that position. "No. I'm not running and I'm not going to run," she said. "I'm in Washington. I've got this really great job and a chance to try and make a difference on things that really matter."[6] For a long time, she held back from endorsing Hillary Clinton because of Clinton's close ties with Wall Street. In the end, however, she threw her support firmly behind the Democratic candidate, giving Clinton her endorsement and making **scathing** comments about the Republican candidate, Donald Trump.

Warren was on Clinton's short list of possible vice presidential candidates. Warren was perceived as a Washington outsider, in contrast to the popular idea that Clinton represented the Washington establishment, which many people felt had let them down. One of Clinton's biggest challenges was convincing fed-up voters that someone who had been in public life for thirty years and had served in Washington would change things for them. Choosing Warren could have provided a boost to Clinton's credibility. During the campaign, according to an NPR report, "Clinton praised Warren, saying that when she is on C-SPAN in Senate hearings pressing bank executives and regulators for answers, 'She is speaking for every American who is frustrated and fed up. She is speaking for all of us, and we thank her for that.'"[7]

Elizabeth Warren appears with Hillary Clinton at a rally during Clinton's 2016 presidential campaign.

Although Clinton ultimately chose Tim Kaine, a senator from Virginia, as her running mate, Warren continued to support her. The principles of the Democrats were dramatically opposed to those of the Republicans, and Warren did everything she could to encourage people to vote for the Democratic ticket. Warren knew that the Republicans were staunch supporters of the banking industry and Wall Street. She understood that a Republican victory would likely lead to a reduction in financial regulations that protect ordinary people. She gave a stirring speech at the Democratic

National Convention, strongly attacking Donald Trump, his rhetoric, and his positions.

> *Trump's entire campaign is just one more late-night Trump infomercial. Hand over your money, your jobs, your children's future, and The Great Trump Hot Air Machine will reveal all the answers. And, for one low, low price, he'll even throw in a goofy hat.*[8]

Elsewhere in the speech, Warren said:

> *Here's the thing: America isn't going broke. The stock market is breaking records. Corporate profits are at all-time highs. CEOs make tens of millions of dollars. There's lots of wealth in America, but it isn't trickling down to hard-working families like yours. Does anyone here have a problem with that? Well, I do too ... When giant companies wanted more tax loopholes, Washington got it done. When huge energy companies wanted to tear up our environment, Washington got it done. When enormous Wall Street banks wanted new regulatory loopholes, Washington got it done. No gridlock there! But try to do something, anything, for working people, and you'll have a fight on your hands ... I'm not someone who thinks Republicans are always wrong and Democrats are always right. There's enough blame to go around. But there is a huge difference between the people fighting for a level playing field, and the people keeping the system rigged.*[9]

Warren went on to reiterate some of her most important points.

- "No matter who you are, no matter where you're from, no matter who you love, equal means equal."

- "No one, no one, who works full time should live in poverty." There should be a raise in the minimum wage and paid family and medical leave.

- "Every kid in America should have a chance for a great education without getting crushed by debt." There should be refinancing of student loans.

- "Seniors should be able to retire with dignity." Social Security should be expanded, Medicare should be strengthened, and retirement accounts should be protected.

- "Oil companies shouldn't call the shots in Washington." Climate change is real and needs to be addressed.

- Women should have equal pay for equal work and control over their own bodies.

- There should be strong regulation of banks, and big banks should be held accountable for their actions.

- "The United States should never, never, sign trade deals that help giant corporations but leave working people in the dirt!"

- "We must get big money out of politics and root out corruption."[10]

In the wake of Hillary Clinton's loss to Donald Trump, many political experts are suggesting that the time is ripe for Warren to step into the void left in Democratic leadership. Many members of the Democratic Party see a need to broaden the party's appeal to younger and working-class voters. This means that that populist members of the party are likely to be front and center in upcoming party activities. Because she is known nationally, and because many voters view her positively, many people see her as the new face of the Democratic Party. So, what does the future hold for Elizabeth Warren?

CHAPTER SIX

What the Future Holds

Elizabeth Warren was the primary sponsor or cosponsor of a large number of bills in the Senate's 2015–2016 session. Warren's popularity with voters is the result of her well-known efforts to protect them and enhance their well-being. With Republicans in control of the Senate, most of Warren's proposed bills never made it out of committee during the 2015–2016 session to receive a full vote on the Senate floor. It's not unusual for bills to "die in committee" like

Elizabeth Warren at work in the Senate, where she faces great opposition from Republicans this, and legislators will often reintroduce a bill in the new session of Congress. Even if Warren's bills don't pass, they represent the issues that she has fought passionately for and will continue to fight for in the future. No doubt Warren will continue to sponsor bills along the same lines.

The Equal Employment for All Act of 2015 would have amended the Fair Credit Reporting Act to prohibit consumer credit reporting agencies from supplying consumers' credit information to an employer for use in making hiring or other employment decisions, unless the job in question required access to classified information or a credit check were required by law for the position. This law would have helped protect people forced into home foreclosures during the financial crisis from being discriminated against.

The Truth in Settlements Act of 2015 would have required information to be released about the amount of money the US government obtained as the result of investigations into wrongdoing. For example, if a federal enforcement agency were investigating a bank, and the bank agreed to pay a fine to settle the case, this bill would have required information to be made available on the actual amount the bank was paying, after any tax deductions or other credits were subtracted from the agreed-upon amount. This measure would have let the public know if companies that violated the law were adequately paying for their transgressions. The 21st Century Glass-Steagall Act of 2015 was designed to reduce risks to the financial system by limiting banks' ability to engage in certain risky activities, and by limiting conflicts of interest. Its purpose was to reinstate certain protections that were included in the original Glass-Steagall Act passed during the Great Depression and later repealed. The idea was to have banks focus on traditional banking activities such as lending money, while reducing their participation in risky stock-trading activities. The Trade Transparency Act of 2015 would have required the president to make the text of trade agreements available to the public in order for those agreements to receive **expedited** consideration from Congress. This bill would have made the terms of trade agreements available to workers who might be affected by them, giving them a chance to influence their legislators. The Bailout Prevention Act of 2015 would have required the Federal Reserve to charge a reasonable interest rate on money lent to banks, keeping the government from using taxpayers' money to subsidize banks that need to be bailed out.

A Future in Party Leadership

Throughout the 2016 presidential campaign, Elizabeth Warren waged a war of words with presidential candidate Donald Trump. After Trump's victory, Warren expressed a willingness to work with the new president, but her tone wasn't exactly **conciliatory**. Speaking to the board of directors of the AFL-CIO labor union, Warren indicated that she would work with Trump if he is serious about improving the lot of the middle class, but:

We will stand up to bigotry. No compromises on this one, ever ... In all its forms, we will fight back against attacks on Latinos, African Americans, women, Muslims, immigrants, disabled Americans—on anyone. Whether Donald Trump sits in a glass tower or sits in the White House, we will not give an inch on this, not now, not ever.[1]

According to reporter Kery Murakami, Warren also stated that "she will fight Trump and the Republicans 'every step of the way' if they tried to hand 'the keys to our economy over to Wall Street so they can run it for themselves.'"[2]

In the days after the election, Elizabeth Warren appeared in public day after day, clearly emerging as one of the Democratic leaders. She made public appearances and issued letters from her Senate office. Although she stated that there are areas where the Democrats can work with Republicans, she has called on members of her party to stand firm against Trump when his actions are against the best interests of ordinary people. David Pepper, chair of the Ohio Democratic Party, stated:

Given what's just happened, there really is a question: Who are the leaders of the party? It's great to see [Warren] doing all that. I can tell you from being on the ground here in Ohio, no one electrifies voters like Elizabeth Warren ... There is a little bit of a void, and I think her voice coming through loud and clear is great.[3]

Following the Democratic loss in the 2016 election, Elizabeth Warren gives a speech on the need to better address the concerns of voters.

One of Warren's goals is to provide the Democrats with a framework from which to talk about issues with the White House. In the days following the 2016 election, she met with major groups that support Democratic positions, such as the AFL-CIO, and with key Democratic organizations, such as the Democracy Alliance donor network and the Congressional Progressive Caucus, to discuss the lessons learned from the election, especially the need to address the economic concerns of voters.

Trump favors deregulation of the banks, which would remove many of the controls that the Democrats placed on them during the Obama administration. For example, Trump's victory endangers the Consumer Financial Protection Bureau. The Republicans want changes that would put the agency under their control. In October of 2016, they succeeded in getting a court of appeals ruling that would allow the director of the agency to be replaced by the president at will. This means that Trump could replace the current director, Richard Cordray, with someone less aggressive about pursuing oversight, before Cordray's term ends in 2018. The CFPB appealed the ruling, stating that it interferes with Congress's ability to create independent agencies and that it could affect other agencies as well, including the Social Security Administration, the Federal Housing Finance Agency, and the Office of Special Counsel. As of this writing, Trump has not specifically mentioned changes to the CFPB, but he has stated that he would like to repeal the Dodd-Frank Act, which resulted in the agency's creation. Trump could potentially ask for legislation that gives Congress control over the CFPB and/or repeals specific agency regulations, such as the one that allows consumers to sue banks.

Warren isn't prepared to sit idly by while Trump guts the agency. According to Warren, "If Trump and the Republican Party try to turn loose the big banks and financial institutions so they can once again gamble with our economy and bring it all crashing down, then we will fight them every step of the way."[4]

No sooner had Trump been elected than Warren sent a letter to him, chastising him for appointing Wall Street insiders and lobbyists to his transition team, the group of people who assist the president-elect in finding people to fill key posts in the administration. The letter, posted on Warren's Facebook page, was viewed over ten million times. It said:

If you truly stand by your commitment to making government work for all Americans—not just those with armies of lobbyists on payroll—you must remove the lobbyists and financial bigwigs from your transition team and reinstate a group of advisors who will fight for the interests of all Americans. Maintaining a transition team of Washington insiders sends a clear signal to all who are watching you—that you are already breaking your campaign promises to "drain the swamp" and that you are selling out the American public.[5]

The day after writing the letter, Warren joined other Democrats in opposing Trump's appointment of Steve Bannon, a known bigot, as his chief strategist. There is some evidence that Warren's attacks on the new president are having an effect. A week after the election, Warren addressed the *Wall Street Journal*'s CEO council, a group consisting of the heads of many of America's largest corporations, saying:

How is Donald Trump going to show that he actually heard that message [of change]? That's the message that he ran on, but right now what he's doing is putting together a transition team that is full of lobbyists and the kind of people he actually ran against. So part of what we have to assess here is "What is the mandate coming out?" And I think that the clearest point that comes out of this election is that the American people do not want Wall Street to run their government. They do not want corporate executives to be the ones calling the shots in Washington. [6]

A day after Warren's speech, Vice President Mike Pence, who was in charge of the transition team, began removing lobbyists from it.

In a June 2016 article in the *Boston Globe*, columnist Joshua Green made the case for Elizabeth Warren as one of the most effective senators in Congress. The article was a rebuttal of a tweet by Donald Trump on May 11, 2016, which said, "Goofy Elizabeth Warren has been one of the least effective senators in the entire US Senate. She has done nothing!" Green begged to differ. In the column, he states, "Warren's effectiveness often can't be measured by standard markers of success, such as the passage of a new law." According to Green, Warren has, in fact, had a tremendous impact on policy in Washington. For example, at one time President Obama wanted to cut Social Security as part of a deal with the Republicans to reduce the deficit. Although some Democrats objected to cuts, no one suggested expanding Social Security. When Warren took her seat in the Senate in 2013, she developed an interest in bills aimed at expanding Social Security, proposed by two Democrats, Senators Tom Harkin of Iowa and Mark Begich of Alaska. She shared her views with liberal activist organizations, and they popularized the idea. In November 2013, she gave a speech in the Senate endorsing the idea. She was actually the seventh senator to do so, but because of her celebrity, her endorsement attracted more attention. Green says:

> She drew a furious response that earlier efforts hadn't occasioned. The centrist Democratic group Third Way attacked her proposal as "reckless." This assault on Warren by "corporate" Democrats galvanized the party's left wing. Suddenly, Democrats were debating expansion. It had moved into the mainstream.[7]

In March 2015, Warren introduced an amendment expanding Social Security to a Senate budget resolution. The measure failed, which was not a surprise, since Republicans had the majority in the Senate. The important aspect of the move was that it forced Democrats to vote on the idea—to take a stand. Forty-two Democratic senators voted "yes," including Bernie

Sanders. When Sanders initiated his presidential election campaign, he made the expansion one of the issues in his platform, in contrast to Hillary Clinton, who didn't support it. As it became clear that Sanders's campaign had garnered immense popular support because of issues like this, pressure increased on Clinton to support expanding, not cutting, Social Security—and by April 2016 the idea became part of her platform. In May 2016, President Obama, in a reversal of his previous position, announced: "It is time we finally [make] Social Security more generous and increase the benefits so that today's retirees and future generations get the dignified retirement they have earned."[8] Elizabeth Warren succeeded in getting a political party and a president to reverse their position on a major issue. This is the kind of force that Warren possesses. It is one reason that many people in the Democratic Party see Warren as the logical successor to Barack Obama and Hillary Clinton as the face of the party.

2018 Reelection Campaign

Warren is a critic of President Donald Trump and the Republican-controlled Congress. In January 2017, Warren announced that she would seek reelection when her current term in the Senate ends in 2018. In making her announcement, she stated:

Fighting for the Future

Warren's future activities in Congress will be the result of her continued fight for the causes that concern her most. During the 2015–2016 session of the Senate, the committees she served on were:

Committee on Banking, Housing, and Urban Affairs: "Senator Warren works on legislation related to financial services and the economy, housing, urban development, and other issues, and participates in oversight of federal regulatory agencies."

Committee on Health, Education, Labor and Pensions (HELP): "Senator Warren is focused on many important issues affecting working families in Massachusetts and across the country, including ensuring access to high-quality affordable health care, making sure every child has access to a good education, strengthening employment protections for workers, and promoting a secure retirement for our nation's seniors."

Special Committee on Aging: "Senator Warren is focused on supporting and strengthening Social Security, Medicare, and other programs essential to older Americans, as well as working to protect seniors from fraud and abuse. Senator Warren is committed to ensuring that everyone has access to a secure and dignified retirement."

Committee on Energy and Natural Resources: "Senator Warren works on issues related to shaping our nation's energy policy, ensuring the responsible development of our natural resources, and overseeing the management of public lands."[9]

With the results of the 2016 elections, Warren is likely to have her work cut out for her. But there is no doubt she will continue to fight to achieve her goals.

> *This isn't the fight we were expecting to fight. But this is the fight that's in front of us. And the people of Massachusetts didn't send me to Washington to roll over and play dead while Donald Trump and his team of billionaires, bigots, and Wall Street bankers crush the working people of our Commonwealth and this country.*[10]

Boston Red Sox pitcher Curt Schilling has already declared that he will run against her, assuming he wins the Republican primary for the Massachusetts Senate race. Schilling is a staunch Trump supporter. In discussing the future, Warren said she expects the fights she faces in her remaining two years in Congress and her future reelection campaign to be "uglier and nastier than anything we've ever imagined."[11]

A Presidential Run?

The *International Business Times* suggested six Democrats as possible candidates to run against Donald Trump in 2020. One of them was Elizabeth Warren. A number of commentators, including filmmaker Michael Moore, have called for activists to take control of the Democratic Party. Bernie Sanders and Elizabeth Warren are generally acknowledged to be the leaders of the populist side of the Democratic Party. Indeed, no sooner had the votes been counted in the 2016 presidential election than social media began to buzz with people suggesting that Warren should run in 2020.

The popularity and power of Elizabeth Warren are not lost on the Democratic Party leadership. In November 2016, Senator Chuck Schumer of New York was voted to replace Harry Reid as Senate minority leader (the head of the party with fewer seats in the Senate) in 2017. He picked Elizabeth Warren to work with him as one of his ten-member Democratic leadership group. The team shapes the Democratic agenda, strategy, and message. Warren's inclusion was an acknowledgment of the size of her following and the influence she has with the public. In discussing his appointments to the team, Schumer told reporters, "We heard the American people loud and clear. They felt that the government wasn't working for them. They felt that the economy was rigged against them in many places and that the government was too beholden to big money and special interests."[12] It's clear that Warren has a reputation for fighting for the economically **dispossessed** and could be an appealing presidential candidate in the future. According to Charles Chamberlain, executive director of Democracy for America, an organization that pushed for Warren to run in the 2016 presidential election, "It's more true than ever that the leaders of our party and the leaders of our movement are going to be Bernie [Sanders] and Elizabeth … It's not going to come from the old Wall Street wing of the party."[13]

As soon as the 2016 election was over, Warren started making speeches that included warnings to both Democrats and Republicans about the dangers of getting too cozy with the Wall Street establishment and failing to respond to the concerns of ordinary people. She has gone on television to make her point. In an interview with Rachel Maddow on MSNBC, she said, "Look, this is painful. This really and truly hurts … But we are going to fight back. We are not turning this country over to what Donald Trump has sold."[14] Having said that, however, she went on to admit that there were areas where the Democrats could work with the new president. Among these are reinstituting a new version of the Glass-Steagall Act, which was passed after the Great Depression but was repealed in 1999. The act restricted the investment activities of banks, which helped keep them from engaging in dangerous speculation. There is also the possibility of working together on raising the minimum wage and protecting Social Security. In addition, Warren suggested that she could work with Trump if he makes positive changes to the Affordable Care Act, better known as Obamacare. She made it clear that she will do everything to block him, however, if he deregulates Wall Street and the banks to the point where they can ruin the economy once again. To many people, the way that Warren has stepped out and articulated what is and is not acceptable makes it appear that she is positioning herself as a party leader. Some political commentators feel she may already be positioning herself to run in the 2020 presidential contest.

Warren is not the only candidate who could take control of the party, however. Senator Bernie Sanders of Vermont, who did an impressive job of inspiring a nationwide movement—especially among young people—is likely to continue to play a major role in the Democratic Party. Sanders hasn't ruled out another run for the presidency in 2020. However, Sanders would be seventy-nine years old if he were elected. Warren would be seventy-one, not tremendously old by today's standards. (Donald Trump, in comparison, was seventy when he was elected president in 2016.) In a 2017 interview with the Associated Press, Warren said she had not ruled out a run for the presidency in 2020. However, she stated that she was not thinking about that yet. [15] As part of potential preparation for a presidential run, in 2017 she took a seat on the Senate Armed Forces Committee, which allows her to build up her foreign policy credentials. Serving on the Armed Forces Committee is a typical move for senators seeking to run for the presidency who have not served in the military.

In her concession speech in the 2016 election, Hillary Clinton stated that, although the "glass ceiling" remains intact for now, someday it will be shattered. It's always possible that 2020 could be the year. Regardless of whether or not she chooses to run for president, Elizabeth Warren started life as girl whose family was barely hanging on in the middle class. Nonetheless, through hard work and incredible perseverance, she has achieved a remarkable series of accomplishments not only personally but for ordinary people. Her accomplishments demonstrate what it is possible for a girl who applies herself to achieve.

Timeline

1968

Elizabeth marries Jim Warren.

1985

Warren becomes a professor at Penn State University.

1978

Elizabeth and Jim Warren divorce.

Elizabeth Herring is born in Oklahoma City, Oklahoma.

June 22, 1949

Warren marries Bruce Mann.

1980

Warren accepts a full-time job as a law professor at Harvard University and joins the National Bankruptcy Review Commission.

Warren graduates from Rutgers University Law School.

1976

1995

2008

Warren becomes a member of the Congressional Oversight Panel (COP) monitoring the Troubled Assets Relief Program (TARP) at the US Treasury.

2012

Warren is elected the first female senator from the Commonwealth of Massachusetts.

Warren's Consumer Financial Protection Bureau becomes a reality when the Dodd-Frank Act is signed into law.

2010

Warren delivers the keynote address at the 2016 Democratic National Convention in Philadelphia, Pennsylvania.

2016

SOURCE NOTES

Chapter 1

1. Pooja Nair, "Insights from Professor Warren: Analyzing Elizabeth Warren's Academic Career," *Bloomberg*, March 15, 2013, http://www.bna.com/insights-from-professor-Warren-analyzing-elizabeth-warrens-academic-career.

2. Harry Kreisler, "Law, Politics, and the Coming Collapse of the Middle Class: Conversation with Elizabeth Warren," University of California, Berkeley, Institute of International Studies, March 8, 2007, http://globetrotter.berkeley.edu/people7/Warren/warren-con0.html.

3. Ibid.

4. Noah Bierman, "A Girl Who Soared, but Longed to Belong," *Boston Globe*, February 12, 2012, http://www.bostonglobe.com/metro/2012/02/12/for-warren-seeds-activism-forged-plains-oklahoma/rx59B8AcqsZokclyJXkg7I/story.html?camp=pm.

5. Kreisler, "Law, Politics, and the Coming Collapse of the Middle Class."

6. Elizabeth Warren, *A Fighting Chance* (New York: Picador, 2015), 10.

7. Ibid., 13.

8. Ibid., 15.

9. Ibid., 16.

Chapter 2

1. "Bankruptcy," Investopedia, Retrieved January 5, 2017, http://www.investopedia.com/terms/b/bankruptcy.asp#ixzz4Sw13Ft4H.

2. Warren, *A Fighting Chance*, 34.

3. Eric Moskowitz, "At Harvard, Elizabeth Warren Has Warm Reputation," *Boston Globe*, October 13, 2012, https://www.bostonglobe.com/metro/2012/10/13/ elizabeth-warren-known-harvard-law-school-tough-but-fair/9adfuU4jXPPSEfO8XyturM/story.html.

4. Warren, *A Fighting Chance*, 43.

Chapter 3

1. Kreisler, "Law, Politics, and the Coming Collapse of the Middle Class."

2. Warren, *A Fighting Chance*, 81.

3. Michael Scherer, "The New Sheriffs of Wall Street," *Time*, May 13, 2010, http://content.time.com/time/magazine/ article/0,9171,1989144,00.html.

4. Suzanna Andrews, "The Woman Who Knew Too Much," *Vanity Fair*, November 2011, http://www.vanityfair.com/ news/2011/11/elizabeth-warren-201111.

5. Ibid.

6. Warren, *A Fighting Chance*, 126.

Chapter 4

1. Warren, *A Fighting Chance*, 158.

2. Erika Eichelberger, "10 Things Elizabeth Warren's Consumer Protection Agency Has Done for You," *Mother Jones*, March 14, 2014, http://www.motherjones.com/politics/2014/02/ elizabeth-warren-consumer-financial-protection-bureau.

3. Brady Dennis, "Elizabeth Warren, Likely to Head New Consumer Agency, Provokes Strong Feelings," *Washington Post*, August 13, 2010, http://www.washingtonpost.com/wp-dyn/content/article/2010/08/12/AR2010081206356.html.

4. Ibid.

5. Ibid.

6. Andy Kroll, "Tim Geithner on Why Obama Passed Over Elizabeth Warren to Head the Consumer Protection Bureau," *Mother Jones*, May 12, 2014, http://www. motherjones.com/mojo/2014/05/tim-geithner-book-obama-elizabeth-warren-consumer-bureau.

7. Ibid.

Chapter 5

1. "Nominations," Oklahoma Hall of Fame, Retrieved January 5, 2017, http://oklahomahof.com/nominations.

2. Warren. *A Fighting Chance*, 215.

3. "Elizabeth Warren's Democratic Convention Speech," ABC News, September 5, 2012, http://abcnews.go.com/ Politics/OTUS/transcript-elizabeth-warrens-democratic-convention-speech/story?id=17164726.

4. Chris Cillizza, "Democratic Convention Night 2: Winners and Losers," *Washington Post*, September 5, 2012, https:// www.washingtonpost.com/news/the-fix/wp/2012/09/05/ democratic-national-convention-night-2-winners-and-losers/?utm_term=.d039574d4b49.

5. Noam Scheiber, "Hillary's Nightmare? A Democratic Party That Realizes Its Soul Lies with Elizabeth Warren," *New Republic*, November 10, 2013, https://newrepublic. com/article/115509/hillarys-nightmare-democratic-party-realizes-soul-lies-elizabeth-warren.

6. Eun Kyung Kim, "Elizabeth Warren on 2016: 'I'm Not Going to Run'—and Hillary Clinton Deserves 'a Chance to Decide,'" Today.com, May 31, 2015, http://www.today.com/ news/elizabeth-warren-2016-i-m-not-going-run-hillary-clinton-t12086.

7. Tamara Keith, "Elizabeth Warren Campaigns with Hillary Clinton, Goes After Donald Trump," NPR, June 27, 2016, http://www.npr.org/2016/06/27/483706454/elizabeth-

warren-campaigns-with-hillary-clinton-goes-after-donald-trump.

8. Will Drabold, "Read Elizabeth Warren's Anti-Trump Speech at the Democratic National Convention," *Time*, July 25, 2016, http://time.com/4421731/democratic-convention-elizabeth-warren-transcript-speech.

9. Ibid.

10. Ibid.

Chapter 6

1. Gabriel Debenedetti, "Elizabeth Warren Fills the Democratic Void," *Politico*, November 21, 2016, http://www.politico.com/story/2016/11/elizabeth-warren-democrats-liberals-231692.

2. Kery Murakami, "Sen. Elizabeth Warren's Future Changed in a Few Short Hours Tuesday," *Claremore Daily Progress*, November 11, 2016, http://www.claremoreprogress.com/cnhi_network/sen-elizabeth-warren-s-future-changed-in-a-few-short/article_2a6bbf6c-069b-52d1-a649-5c732d756e56.html.

3. Debenedetti, "Elizabeth Warren Fills the Democratic Void."

4. Elizabeth Dexheimer, "Warren Says She Would Work with Trump on Bank-Industry Policies," *Bloomberg*, November 10, 2016, http://www.bloomberg.com/news/articles/2016-11-10/warren-says-she-would-work-with-trump-on-bank-industry-policies.

5. Elizabeth Warren, letter to Donald Trump, November 15, 2016, http://www.warren.senate.gov/files/documents/2016-11-15-Trump_Letter.pdf.

6. Debenedetti, "Elizabeth Warren Fills the Democratic Void."

7. Joshua Green, "Trump's Flat-Out Wrong About Elizabeth Warren's Senate Record," *Boston Globe*, June 7, 2016, https://www.bostonglobe.com/opinion/2016/06/07/contra-

trump-elizabeth-warren-one-most-effective-senators/
SOiAYippio2rybOEQZqqVL/story.html.

8. Ibid.

9. "Committees," Elizabeth Warren's Senate website, Retrieved January 5, 2017, https://www.warren.senate. gov/?p=committees.

10. Bob Salsberg, "Elizabeth Warren Announces Run for Senate Re-election in 2018," WBUR News, January 6, 2017, http:// www.wbur.org/news/2017/01/06/elizabeth-warren-running-reelection.

11. Ibid.

12. Susan Milligan, "Sanders, Warren Tapped for Democratic Leadership Posts," *US News and World Report*, November 16, 2016, http://www.usnews.com/news/articles/2016-11-16/ bernie-sanders-elizabeth-warren-on-senate-democrats-expanded-leadership-team.

13. Michael Levenson and Annie Linskey, "Elizabeth Warren, Bernie Sanders Duo Will Lead Liberals in the Senate," *Boston Globe*, November 12, 2016, https://www.bostonglobe. com/metro/2016/11/11/elizabeth-warren-bernie-sanders-duo-will-lead-liberals-senate/vjyyHGz38b5ct4w1FIFp4N/ story.html.

14. Ciro Scotti, "Elizabeth Warren Is Already Positioning Herself for 2020," *Fiscal Times*, November 11, 2016, http:// www.thefiscaltimes.com/2016/11/11/Elizabeth-Warren-Next-Leader-Democratic-Party.

15. Salsberg, "Elizabeth Warren Announces Run for Senate Re-election in 2018."

GLOSSARY

affirmatively In agreement with.

audiology The study of hearing

bipartisanship Cooperation between both parties, such as the Democrats and the Republicans.

brouhaha Turmoil.

conciliatory Agreeable, making up for differences of opinion.

counterfactual In opposition to the facts.

deregulation To remove the regulations from.

dispossessed Without property or status.

empathy Having a sense of what another person is feeling.

expedited To accomplish more quickly than usual.

Federal Reserve The central government bank of the United States.

foreclosure The process by which a bank takes possession of a house.

populist Appealing to the people, rather than the elite.

precipitous Steep.

scathing Sharp and severe.

speech pathology The study of speaking disorders.

tenure The granting of a permanent position, especially at a college or university.

Troubled Assets Relief Program (TARP) A program instituted by the government after the 2008 financial crisis. The government provided money to banks to keep them from failing.

FURTHER INFORMATION

Books

Carr, Ruth. *Elizabeth Warren: Understanding the Life and Teachings of Elizabeth Warren*. Published by the author, 2015.

Etheridge, Emily. *Powerful Women: The 25 Most Influential Women in Congress*. Washington, DC: CQ Roll Call, 2015.

Freedman, Jeri. *The US Economic Crisis*. In the News. New York: Rosen Publishing, 2010.

Web Sites

Elizabeth Warren for Massachusetts
http://www.elizabethwarren.com

This site includes a blog written by Warren, which details her latest concerns and commentary on national events.

Elizabeth Warren on Facebook
https://www.facebook.com/ElizabethWarren

This site provides videos and photos of Elizabeth Warren, as well as news about her.

Elizabeth Warren's Senate Website
http://www.warren.senate.gov

Elizabeth Warren's Senate website provides information on all her activities.

Huffington Post: **Elizabeth Warren**
http://www.huffingtonpost.com/news/elizabeth-warren

The *Huffington Post* Elizabeth Warren page includes articles and commentary about Elizabeth Warren.

New York Times: **Elizabeth Warren**
http://www.nytimes.com/topic/person/elizabeth-warren

The *New York Times* Elizabeth Warren page contains news about Warren, including commentary and archived articles.

Video

Charlie Rose—Elizabeth Warren
This DVD features an in-depth interview with Elizabeth Warren.

BIBLIOGRAPHY

Andrews, Suzanna. "The Woman Who Knew Too Much." *Vanity Fair*, November 2011. http://www.vanityfair.com/ news/2011/11/elizabeth-warren-201111.

"Bankruptcy." Investopedia. Retrieved January 5, 2017. http://www.investopedia.com/terms/b/bankruptcy. asp#ixzz4Sw13Ft4H.

Bierman, Noah. "A Girl Who Soared, but Longed to Belong." *Boston Globe*, February 12, 2012. http://www.bostonglobe. com/metro/2012/02/12/for-warren-seeds-activism-forged-plains-oklahoma/rx59B8AcqsZokclyJXkg7I/story. html?camp=pm.

Bierman, Noah, and Frank Phillips. "Elizabeth Warren Defeats Scott Brown." *Boston Globe*, November 7, 2012. https:// www.bostonglobe.com/metro/2012/11/07/elizabeth-warren-defeats-incumbent-scott-brown-first-mass-woman-senate-hard-race-ends-victory-for-liberalism/ i0PsriZIRzoiQPrQtjCxML/story.html.

Blake, Aaron. "Why Elizabeth Warren Is Perfectly Positioned for 2016 (If She Wanted to Run)." *Washington Post*, May 1, 2014. https://www.washingtonpost.com/news/the-fix/ wp/2014/05/01/why-elizabeth-warren-could-definitely-run-for-president-if-she-wanted-to/?utm_term=.07a9add0b891.

Cillizza, Chris. "Democratic Convention Night 2: Winners and Losers." *Washington Post*, September 5, 2012. https:// www.washingtonpost.com/news/the-fix/wp/2012/09/05/ democratic-national-convention-night-2-winners-and-losers/?utm_term=.d039574d4b49.

Debenedetti, Gabriel. "Elizabeth Warren Fills the Democratic Void." *Politico*, November 21, 2016. http://www.politico.com/story/2016/11/elizabeth-warren-democrats-liberals-231692.

Dennis, Brady. "Elizabeth Warren, Likely to Head New Consumer Agency, Provokes Strong Feelings." *Washington Post*, August 13, 2010. http://www.washingtonpost.com/wp-dyn/content/article/2010/08/12/AR2010081206356.html.

Dexheimer, Elizabeth. "Warren Says She Would Work with Trump on Bank-Industry Policies." *Bloomberg*, November 10, 2016. http://www.bloomberg.com/news/articles/2016-11-10/warren-says-she-would-work-with-trump-on-bank-industry-policies.

Drabold, Will. "Read Elizabeth Warren's Anti-Trump Speech at the Democratic National Convention." *Time*, July 25, 2016. http://time.com/4421731/democratic-convention-elizabeth-warren-transcript-speech.

Ebbert, Stephanie. "Family Long a Bedrock for Warren." *Boston Globe*, October 25, 2012. http://archive.boston.com/news/politics/2012/10/24/elizabeth-warren-family/v0IZ9AryRoiaOyY61vKM3O/story.html.

Ebbert, Stephanie, and Michael Levenson. "For Professor Warren, a Steep Climb." Boston.com, August 19, 2012. http://archive.boston.com/news/politics/2012/senate/2012/08/19/warren-career-story/08IJlqnGKaRYzIgKNMmVbM/singlepage.html.

Eichelberger, Erika. "10 Things Elizabeth Warren's Consumer Protection Agency Has Done for You." *Mother Jones*, March 14, 2014. http://www.motherjones.com/politics/2014/02/elizabeth-warren-consumer-financial-protection-bureau.

"Elizabeth Warren." Biography.com. Retrieved October 26, 2016. http://www.biography.com/people/elizabeth-warren-20670753.

"Elizabeth Warren's Democratic Convention Speech." ABC
News, September 5, 2012. http://abcnews.go.com/
Politics/OTUS/transcript-elizabeth-warrens-democratic-
convention-speech/story?id=17164726.

"Elizabeth Warren, US Senator from Massachusetts." Retrieved
January 5, 2017. https://www.warren.senate.gov.

Fulton, Deirdre. "Trump and GOP Set to Eviscerate Warren's
Consumer Protection Agency." Common Dreams,
November 11, 2016. http://www.commondreams.org/
news/2016/11/11/trump-and-gop-set-eviscerate-warrens-
consumer-protection-agency.

Green, Joshua. "Trump's Flat-Out Wrong About Elizabeth
Warren's Senate Record. *Boston Globe*, June 7, 2016. https://
www.bostonglobe.com/opinion/2016/06/07/contra-
trump-elizabeth-warren-one-most-effective-senators/
SOiAYippio2rybOEQZqqVL/story.html.

Keith, Tamara. "Elizabeth Warren Campaigns with Hillary
Clinton, Goes After Donald Trump." NPR, June 27, 2016.
http://www.npr.org/2016/06/27/483706454/elizabeth-
warren-campaigns-with-hillary-clinton-goes-after-donald-
trump.

Kim, Eun Kyung. "Elizabeth Warren on 2016: 'I'm Not Going
to Run'—and Hillary Clinton Deserves 'a Chance to
Decide.'" Today.com, May 31, 2015. http://www.today.com/
news/elizabeth-warren-2016-i-m-not-going-run-hillary-
clinton-t12086.

Kirchgaessner, Stephanie. "Warren Attacks CEOs Who
'Wrecked Economy.'" *Financial Times*, September 6, 2012.
https://web.archive.org/web/20120908033052/http://www.
ft.com/cms/s/0/5718c926-f7d4-11e1-ba54-00144feabdc0.
html#axzz4OFHUmehd.

Kreisler, Harry. "Law, Politics, and the Coming Collapse of
the Middle Class: Conversation with Elizabeth Warren."

University of California, Berkeley, Institute of International Studies, March 8, 2007. http://globetrotter.berkeley.edu/people7/Warren/warren-con0.html.

Kroll, Andy. "Tim Geithner on Why Obama Passed Over Elizabeth Warren to Head the Consumer Protection Bureau." *Mother Jones*, May 12, 2014. http://www.motherjones.com/mojo/2014/05/tim-geithner-book-obama-elizabeth-warren-consumer-bureau.

Levenson, Michael, and Annie Linskey. "Elizabeth Warren, Bernie Sanders Duo Will Lead Liberals in the Senate." *Boston Globe*, November 12, 2016. https://www.bostonglobe.com/metro/2016/11/11/elizabeth-warren-bernie-sanders-duo-will-lead-liberals-senate/vjyyHGz38b5ct4w1FIFp4N/story.html.

Limbaugh, Rush. "Elizabeth Warren Video: One of the Great Teaching Tools on Liberalism." *The Rush Limbaugh Show*, September 22, 2011. http://www.rushlimbaugh.com/daily/2011/09/22/elizabeth_warren_video_one_of_the_great_teaching_tools_on_liberalism.

Marshall, Frank, ed. *Quotable Elizabeth Warren*. New York: Skyhorse Publishing, 2014.

Milligan, Susan. "Sanders, Warren Tapped for Democratic Leadership Posts." *US News and World Report*, November 16, 2016. http://www.usnews.com/news/articles/2016-11-16/bernie-sanders-elizabeth-warren-on-senate-democrats-expanded-leadership-team.

Montopoli, Brian. "Elizabeth Warren Assigned to Senate Banking Committee." CBS News, December 12, 2012. http://www.cbsnews.com/news/elizabeth-warren-assigned-to-senate-banking-committee.

Moskowitz, Eric. "At Harvard, Elizabeth Warren Has Warm Reputation." *Boston Globe*, October 13, 2012. https://www.bostonglobe.com/metro/2012/10/13/

elizabeth-warren-known-harvard-law-school-tough-but-
fair/9adfuU4jXPPSEfO8XyturM/story.html.

Murakami, Kery. "Sen. Elizabeth Warren's Future Changed
in a Few Short Hours Tuesday." *Claremore Daily Progress*,
November 11, 2016. http://www.claremoreprogress.com/
cnhi_network/sen-elizabeth-warren-s-future-changed-in-a-
few-short/article_2a6bbf6c-069b-52d1-a649-5c732d756e56.
html.

Nair, Pooja. "Insights from Professor Warren: Analyzing
Elizabeth Warren's Academic Career." *Bloomberg*, March 15,
2013. http://www.bna.com/insights-from-professor-warren-
analyzing-elizabeth-warrens-academic-career.

Nanos, Janelle. "How'd Elizabeth Warren Do at the DNC?"
Boston Magazine, September 6, 2012. http://www.
bostonmagazine.com/news/blog/2012/09/06/elizabeth-
warren-dnc-speech.

"Nominations." Oklahoma Hall of Fame. Retrieved January 5,
2017. http://oklahomahof.com/nominations.

"President Obama Names Elizabeth Warren Assistant to
the President and Special Advisor to the Secretary of the
Treasury on the Consumer Financial Protection Bureau."
White House Office of the Press Secretary, September
17, 2010. https://www.whitehouse.gov/the-press-
office/2010/09/17/president-obama-names-elizabeth-
warren-assistant-president-and-special-a.

Salsberg, Bob. "Elizabeth Warren Announces Run for Senate
Re-election in 2018." WBUR News, January 6, 2017. http://
www.wbur.org/news/2017/01/06/elizabeth-warren-running-
reelection.

Scheiber, Noam. "Hillary's Nightmare? A Democratic Party
That Realizes Its Soul Lies with Elizabeth Warren." *New
Republic*, November 10, 2013. https://newrepublic.com/

article/115509/hillarys-nightmare-democratic-party-realizes-soul-lies-elizabeth-warren.

Scherer, Michael. "The New Sheriffs of Wall Street." *Time*, May 13, 2010. http://content.time.com/time/magazine/article/0,9171,1989144,00.html.

Scotti, Ciro. "Elizabeth Warren Is Already Positioning Herself for 2020." *Fiscal Times*, November 11, 2016. http://www.thefiscaltimes.com/2016/11/11/Elizabeth-Warren-Next-Leader-Democratic-Party.

"Sen. Elizabeth Warren." *Huffington Post*. Retrieved October 26, 2016. http://www.huffingtonpost.com/author/elizabeth-warren.

Tao, Byron. "Elizabeth Warren Criticizes Donald Trump Over Lobbyists in Transition Team." *Wall Street Journal*, November 15, 2016. http://blogs.wsj.com/washwire/2016/11/15/elizabeth-warren-criticizes-donald-trump-over-lobbyists-in-transition-team.

Thys, Fred. "Elizabeth Warren Sworn In as First Female Senator from Mass." WBUR, Janary 4, 2013. http://legacy.wbur.org/2013/01/04/warren-first-women-senator.

Warren, Elizabeth. *A Fighting Chance*. New York: Picador, 2015.

Williams, Juan. "Juan Williams: Hey Bernie Sanders and Elizabeth Warren, the Democratic Party Is Now Yours for the Taking." Fox News Opinion, November 14, 2016. http://www.foxnews.com/opinion/2016/11/14/juan-williams-hey-bernie-sanders-and-elizabeth-warren-democratic-party-is-now-yours-for-taking.html.

INDEX

Page numbers in **boldface** are illustrations. Entries in **boldface** are glossary terms.

affirmatively, 72
AFL-CIO, 44, 57, 81, 83
audiology, 11

banking industry, 6, 26–28, 32–33, 35–45, 47–49, 51, 54–56, 70, 72–76, 80–81, 83–84, 92
bankruptcy, 20–23, 26–29, 31–33, 35
bipartisanship, 39
brouhaha, 65
Brown, Scott, 59, 63, **64**, 65, 69

Clinton, Hillary, 33, 73–74, **74**, 77, 88, 93
conciliatory, 81
Congressional Oversight Panel, 38–44, **39**, 51, 53, 58
Consumer Financial Protection Bureau, 43–45, 47–59, 84
counterfactual, 72
credit cards, 23, 27, 34, 43–45, 51–52, 55

deregulation, 27, 83, 92
dispossessed, 91
Dodd-Frank Act, 49–52, 84
Dust Bowl, 6

empathy, 8
expedited, 81

Federal Reserve, 27, 70, 81
financial crisis (2008), 26–27, 35–38, **36**, 41, 43–44, 50, 73, 80
foreclosure, 37, 44, 54, 80

Geithner, Timothy, 53, 58–59
George Washington University, 11–12
Great Depression, 6, 37, 81, 92

Harvard University, 24, 28–29, 31, 51, 53, 63, 66
Houston, University of, 12, **13**, 18, 20

interest rates, 26–27, 43, 45, 48, 51, 54, 81

Kennedy, Ted, 32–33, 49, 63

Mann, Bruce, 19–21, 23–24, 28–29, 53
mortgages, 8, 23, 26, 35–37, 43, 45, 51–52, 54

National Bankruptcy Review Commission, 31–33

Obama, Barack, **46**, 51–53, 56–59, **56**, 84, 86, 88

populist, 72, 77, 90
precipitous, 37

Sanders, Bernie, 87–88, 90–93
scathing, 73
Social Security, 76, 84, 86–89, 92
speech pathology, 11
Synar, Mike, **30**, 31

tenure, 18
Troubled Assets Relief Program (TARP), 37–38, 42, 44, 51, 58
Trump, Donald, 73, 75, 77, 81–86, 88, 90, 92–93

Warren, Amelia, 12–15, 34–35, 57
Warren, Elizabeth
  awards and honors, 24, 28, **60**, 61–62

books, 15, 28, 34–35, 40–41, 48–49, 52, 64–65
childhood, **4**, 5–10
Congressional Oversight Panel and, 38–44, **39**, 51, 58
Consumer Financial Protection Bureau and, 43–45, 47–53, 56–59
education, 10–12, 14–15
marriages, 12–14, 18–20
National Bankruptcy Review Commission and, 31–33
Native American controversy, 65–66
presidential run, 69, 72–73, 90–93
research, 21–23, 26–28
Senate campaign, 59, 62–70
Senate work, 70–73, **71**, **78**, 79–81, 84–93
teaching, **16**, 17–21, 23–24, 28–29, 31–32, 51
2016 election and, **67**, 72–77, **74**, 81–83, **83**, 88, 91–92
Warren, Jim, 10, 12–14, 18–19

ABOUT THE AUTHOR

Jeri Freedman has a BA from Harvard University. She is the author of numerous nonfiction books, including *America Debates: Civil Liberties and Terrorism*, *In the News: The US Economic Crisis*, and *Hillary Rodham Clinton: Portrait of a Leading Democrat*.